PRIMERS

The Embodied Image

PRIMERS

The Embodied Image

Imagination and Imagery in Architecture

JUHANI PALLASMAA

WILEY

A John Wiley and Sons, Ltd, Publication

This edition first published 2011

© 2011 John Wiley & Sons Ltd

Registered office

John Wiley & Sons Ltd, The Atrium, Southern Gate, Chichester, West Sussex, PO19 8SQ, United Kingdom

For details of our global editorial offices, for customer services and for information about how to apply for permission to reuse the copyright material in this book please see our website at www.wiley.com.

Executive Commissioning Editor: Helen Castle

Project Editor: Miriam Swift

Assistant Editor: Calver Lezama

ISBN   978-0-470-71191-0 (hb)
            978-0-470-71190-3 (pb)

Series design and cover design by Karen Willcox for aleatoria.com

Page layouts by Sparks Publishing Services Ltd – www.sparkspublishing.com

Printed in Italy by Printer Trento s.r.l

Acknowledgements

The Embodied Image: Imagination and Imagery in Architecture completes my study on the role of the senses, embodiment and imagination in architectural and artistic perception, thought and making. This interest emerged 15 years ago in my critique of the hegemony of vision and the neglected architectural potential of the other senses, entitled *The Eyes of the Skin: Architecture and the Senses* (Academy Editions, London, 1995, and, John Wiley & Sons, London, 2005). This investigation was expanded in *The Thinking Hand: Existential and Embodied Wisdom in Architecture* (John Wiley & Sons, London, 2009) to a study on the significance of the eye–hand–mind connection, regrettably undervalued in the pedagogical and professional practices of the computer age.

Various chapters of the book are partly based on arguments developed in some of my previous lectures and essays, especially the following:

'Hapticity and Time: Notes on Fragile Architecture', first given as the 1999 RIBA Annual Discourse Lecture of The Royal Institute of British Architects in London, and subsequently published in *The Architectural Review* (London), May 2000.

'The Lived Metaphor' in *Primary Architectural Images*: *Seminar Document 2001/2002*, School of Architecture, Washington University in St Louis (St Louis), 2002.

'Aesthetic and Existential Space: The Dialectics of Art and Architecture', *Architecture + Art: New Visions, New Strategies*, Eeva-Liisa Pelkonen, editor, Alvar Aalto Academy (Helsinki), 2007.

'Limits of Architecture: Between Reality and Fiction', lecture at the 11th International Alvar Aalto Symposium, Jyväskylä, 7–9 August 2009.

For the sake of complete argumentation, I have also included a few ideas from my previous book **The Thinking Hand: Existential and Embodied Wisdom in Architecture**. I wish to confess that my thinking seems to advance in slowly enlarging circles, and these concentric patterns require constant return to previous ideas and themes, although each time in a slightly different context and wider view.

As I write everything in longhand, all my manuscripts make on average 8 to 10 rounds between my desk and my secretary's computer; I thank my secretary Arja Riihimäki for her patience and endurance.

I want to thank Helen Castle, Executive Commissioning Editor on the UK Architecture list at John Wiley & Sons for having had the confidence to commission this book on the basis of a single conversation in London in November 2009, as well as her most valuable comments and suggestions on the manuscript. I wish also to thank the following persons who have assisted in the production of this book in various roles: Miriam Swift for her work overseeing the copyediting, design and printing of the book; Julia Dawson for her understanding and careful copyediting; Caroline Ellerby for all the picture research; Karen Willcox for the design; and Calver Lezama for her general assistance and help liaising on the project.

I gave the first draft of my manuscript as a hesitant lecture in March 2010 to a discussion group of artist and scholar friends of mine that meets a few times a year in Helsinki, and received inspiring suggestions.

Whatever I lecture on or write about is an accumulation of reading thousands of books during more than half a century, and of my innumerable conversations in Finland as well as on my travels around the world with artists, philosophers, therapists, scientists and architect colleagues. I have embodied and fused these conversations in my thinking to the degree that individual sources can no longer be identified and credited. This leaves me with the alternative of simply thanking my countless friends collectively.

Helsinki, July 2010
Juhani Pallasmaa

An 'Image' is that which presents an intellectual and emotional complex in an instant of time. Only such an image, such a poetry, could give us that sense of sudden liberation; that sense of freedom from time limits and space limits; that sense of sudden growth, which we experience in the presence of the greatest works of art.

Ezra Pound (As quoted in JD McClatchy, 'Introduction', in *Poets on Painters*, JD McClatchy, editor, University of California Press (Berkeley, Los Angeles, London), 1988, p XI.)

How can an image, at times very unusual, appear to be a concentration of the entire psyche? How – with no preparation – can this singular, short-lived event constituted by the appearance of an unusual poetic image, react on other minds and in other hearts, despite all the barriers of common sense, all the disciplined schools of thought, content in their immobility?

Gaston Bachelard (*The Poetics of Space*, Beacon Press (Boston), 1969, pp XIV–XV.)

We may [...] conclude that imagination is not an empirical power added to consciousness, but it is the whole of consciousness as it realizes its freedom.

Jean-Paul Sartre (*The Imaginary*, Routledge (London and New York), 2004, title page.)

Contents

Introduction

In knowledge imagination serves the understanding
whereas in art understanding serves the imagination.[1]

Immanuel Kant, quoted in Maurice Merleau-Ponty, *Sense and Non-Sense*, 1948

In everyday language the words 'image' and 'imagination' are commonly
used without a deeper thought about their meaning and significance. Yet,
mental imagery is the crucial vehicle of perception, thought, language and
memory. And imagination is not only the somewhat frivolous capability of
daydreaming, as it can be regarded as the foundation of our very humanity.
Thanks to our imagination we are able to grasp the multiplicity of the world
and the continuum of experience through time and life. Without imagination
we would not have our sense of empathy and compassion, or an inkling of
the future. Neither could we make ethical judgements and choices. We must
conclude that our multifaceted image of the world is a product of our own
imagination. 'All reality is brought forth solely by imagination ... this act which
forms the basis for the possibility of our consciousness, our life', philosopher JG
Fichte acknowledges.[2]

The reality of language dominates daily human awareness and communication,
but we are not usually aware of the fact that even language is grounded in
embodied metaphors, images and neural representations. The hegemony of
the word and language is unconsciously and deeply rooted in the traditions
of Western culture and thought in the same way that the unchallenged

hegemony of vision dominates the realms of the other senses. It seems paradoxical that as our cultural practices today are dominated by the sense of vision, at the same time, a biased logocentric view rules over visual imagery, and embodied knowledge in general. The current mass production of commodified and passivating images, that imagine on our behalf, even seems to threaten our authentic capacities of imagination.

Due to the limitless production and commodification of images, the notion 'image' is often taken merely as a shallow and fashionable surface of visual communication and artistic representation. Besides, the notion is often given an instantaneous or momentary character. This disparaging attitude is particularly strong in the field of architecture where 'an architecture of image' commonly denotes a calculating use of architectural faculties for the purposes of creating a seductive and memorable formal configuration, an architectural trademark or signature, as it were. Yet, the most deeply existentially and experientially rooted architectural experiences impact our minds through images which are condensations of distinct architectural essences. Lasting architectural experiences consist of lived and embodied images which have become an inseparable part of our lives.

Special categories of imagery are the poetic and embodied image which are the ground and medium of all artistic expression. The poeticised image is a magical mental act, a shift and transference of awareness which becomes embodied as part of our life world and ourselves. It is a phenomenon of mental alchemy that gives a monumental value to the worthless. As William Carlos Williams observes, 'It is difficult to get the news from poems, yet men die miserably every day for lack of what is found there.'[3]

It is evident that no artistic experience or impact can take place without the mediating faculty of the image that evokes and maintains emotional reaction. The embodied image is a spatialised, materialised and multi-sensory lived experience. Poetic images simultaneously evoke an imaginative reality and become part of our existential experience and sense of self. As they are embodied, they are permitted a decisive role in our inner mental world, the *Weltinnenraum,* to use a notion of Rainer Maria Rilke.[4]

It is yet another paradox of our surreally materialist consumer culture that the authenticity of the image and the autonomy of human imagination are waning. Consequently, at the same time that we need to criticise the exploitative imagery of our mode of culture, for instance, today's forceful architecture of the image, we also have to defend the poetic and embodied image and underline its central role in all artistic experience and thought.

The poeticised world is a familiar, intimate and personal world identified with one's sense of self. As Gaston Bachelard, the philosopher of the poetic image par excellence confesses: 'The image offered us by reading the poem now becomes really our own. It takes root in us. It has been given us by another, but we begin to have the impression that we could have created it, that we should have created it.'[5] Indeed, the imaginative artistic reality *is* of our own projection and creation. Embodied poetic images permit us to experience our own mental emotions through the sensibilities of some of the wisest and most subtle individuals of humankind.

•

I wrote the first drafts of this third book under the working title *The Poetic Image*. However, I was uneasy with its too direct literary and Bachelardian association. In April 2010, I was invited by the Imagine Fund of the University of Minnesota to have six public conversations with the American playwright and theatre director Leigh Fondakowski on seminal issues in the arts. The topics of our conversations were: 1, Image and Meaning; 2, Tradition and Novelty; 3, Time and Timelessness; 4, Reality and Fiction; 5, Anonymity and Expression; and 6, Imagination and Compassion. These spontaneous conversations that took place in various auditoria and theatre venues in Minneapolis and Duluth, made me shift the emphasis of my manuscript to the notion 'embodied'.

The surprising commonalities between the art forms of theatre and architecture, that emerged in the conversations, strengthened my view that artistic imagery from music and poetry, painting and sculpture, to theatre and architecture, acquires its special and magical power through becoming part of the listener/reader/viewer/dweller's embodied existence and sense of self. The real gives rise to an imaginative experience which finally returns back to the life world. The unexpected and largely unexplainable perceptual and emotive power of the artistic image suggests to me that it is deeply grounded in our biological historicity, collective unconscious and existential consciousness.

The book proper begins with a short survey (Chapter 1) into the frequently controversial and even paradoxical role of the image in contemporary culture. The next chapter presents basic observations of the traditionally suppressed status of the image in Western theories of language as well as in the prevailing philosophical traditions. Chapter 3 analyses the multiple faces of the image and, particularly, its mediating role between the world and the realms of thought and imagination. Chapter 4 dissects the anatomy of the image, particularly its dual existence, mental historicity and its relation with time and the concept of beauty. The final, fifth, chapter is engaged with specifically architectural imagery and its mediating and structuring task in human experience and consciousness.

References

1 As quoted in Maurice Merleau-Ponty, 'The Film and the New Psychology', in Maurice Merleau-Ponty, *Sense and Non-Sense* (1948), Northwestern University Press (Evanston, IL), 1991, sixth printing, p 57.
2 As quoted in Richard Kearney, *Poetics of Imagining: From Husserl to Lyotard*, Harper Collins Academic (London), 1991, p 4.
3 William Carlos Williams, 'Asphodel, That Greeny Flower', in *The Collected Poems of William Carlos Williams, Vol 2, 1939–62*, New Directions (New York), 1988, p 318.
4 Liisa Enwald, editor, 'Lukijalle' ['To the Reader'] in Rainer Maria Rilke, *Hiljainen taiteen sisin: kirjeitä vuosilta 1900–1926* [*The Silent Innermost Core of Art: Letters 1900–1926*], TAI-teos (Helsinki), 1997, p 8.
5 Gaston Bachelard, *The Poetics of Space* (1958), Beacon Press (Boston), 1964, p XIX.

1
Image in contemporary culture

One of the greatest paradoxes of contemporary culture is that at a time when the image reigns supreme the very notion of a creative human imagination seems under mounting threat. We no longer appear to know who exactly produces or controls the images which condition our consciousness.[1]

Richard Kearney, *The Wake of Imagination*, 1994

In today's world of mass consumerism, globalisation, worldwide economies and accelerated communication, we are ceaselessly bombarded by visual images. Italo Calvino refers to this experiential condition as 'the unending rainfall of images',[2] whereas Richard Kearney uses the notion 'image addiction'.[3] Roland Barthes calls our entire post-industrial and post-modern mass-media culture 'the civilization of the image'.[4] Today's profusion of images often gives rise to an oppressive feeling of excess and eutrophication, a kind of suffocation in an endless Sargasso Sea of Images.

The constantly developing imaging technologies have certainly opened up entirely new means of monitoring, recording, analysing and depicting countless aspects of reality, and the industrial production of images has made them present anywhere and available to anyone. The image has changed the ways we experience the world and communicate about it. At the same time, the current hegemony of the image has also made its negative impacts apparent.

Hegemony of the image

Images are produced and deployed ad infinitum for purposes of information, education and entertainment, as well as for commercial, ideological and political manipulation, and artistic expression. Our physical world, cityscapes and natural settings, as well as our inner mental landscapes are all colonised today by the image industry. Even the traditional culture of the book seems to have been swiftly replaced by the image and digital information. Recent studies have alarmingly shown the decline of language skills and literary knowledge even in the economically most advanced nations. Before the emergence of the era of writing and mass literacy, humans communicated primarily through gestures and images. Are we now on our way back to a new illiterate age of communicating through the image? Is reading turning into an antiquated skill and a nostalgic pastime of the privileged few?

The excessive flow of imagery gives rise to an experience of a discontinuous and displaced world. In the book, information is usually embedded in long causal narratives, whereas the digital search media mostly provide quick but detached and fragmented pieces of knowledge. A recent study revealed that more than 50 per cent of American children under 15 years old had never watched a single television programme from the beginning to its end.[5] Does this signal the end of complete narratives and the ethics of causation? What is the ethical message of interrupted and discontinuous narratives? As a teacher of architecture I have witnessed the negative impact of easily available but fragmentary information in student papers that tend to lay out numerous facts but often lack an understanding of the essence of the subject. Information is replacing knowledge.

An instant and effortless impact is surely the objective of most of today's communication and entertainment. Even architecture – the art form that, in the view of Sir Christopher Wren in 1660, should bear 'The Attribute of the

eternal', and be 'the only thing incapable of new fashions'[6] – has become an
area of short-lived imagery. This observation is reinforced when comparing
architectural journals from the era of modernity with today's magazines; the
first give the impression of an evolving culture of construction whereas the
latter usually seem to show momentary and individualistic formal inventions.
No wonder, many philosophers of post-modernity have characterised our era
with such words as 'contrived depthlessness', 'waning of historicity and affect'
and 'lacking of overall views'.[7]

At the same time that images have multiplied in number, they have changed
in character. Instead of being representations of a reality, today's forceful
imagery creates its own reality that is often more 'real' than the existing
physical and human worlds. As Richard Kearney suggests, the role of the
image today differs fundamentally from former times, as 'now the image
precedes the reality it is supposed to represent',[8] and 'reality has become a
pale reflection of the image'.[9] Indeed, in today's ordinary life, and commercial
and political practices, as well as the entire expanding realm of entertainment,
the image often dominates or replaces reality, and 'the real and the imaginary
have become almost impossible to distinguish'.[10] The reality of politics today is
most often based on carefully controlled imagery rather than any historically
authenticated truth. In the virtual image world, as in computer games and
virtual reality, or in the simulated surrogate reality of Second Life, the reality
of computer-generated imagery has already replaced the reality of the flesh.
The virtual worlds are already objects of our identity and empathy. In fact, the
notion of 'reality' has been totally relativised; we need to specify whose reality,
and in which context, we are talking about. 'Reality' itself is philosophically a
highly disputable notion, but it has never been as ambiguous and groundless
as today.

The demise of imagination

The notions 'image' and 'imagination' seem to be semantically closely related.
Yet, Kearney reports that many commentators today speak of 'the demise of
imagination'. He makes the further alarming suggestion that 'the very notion
of imaginative creativity may soon be a thing of the past'.[11] In addition to the
fragmentation of information, the increasing speed and short attention span,
and the consequent simplification of both text and image, the accelerated
communication inevitably reduces nuances and flattens the space of individual
imagination. In the case that our autonomous capacities of imagination

and critical judgement would actually weaken, as has been suggested, it is inevitable that our experiences and behaviour are in danger of being increasingly conditioned by images of unidentifiable origins and intentions. The weakening of imagination also suggests a consequent weakening of our empathetic and ethical sense.

Recent neurological studies have greatly advanced the understanding of our brain and neural processes in perceiving, recalling and imagining images, but even this advanced research information is already utilised for the purposes of developing increasingly canny strategies and methods in advertising and commercial conditioning.[12]

At the same time, imagination as an autonomous mental faculty seems to be replaced rather than stimulated by the excessive but passivating external imagery around us. Concerned studies of the influence of the Internet on our cognition have already appeared, such as Nicholas Carr's 'Is Google Making Us Stupid?'. In the writer's view:

> The Internet is likely to have very far-reaching effects on human cognition. Never has a communications system played so many roles in our lives – or exerted such broad influence over our thoughts – as the Internet does today. Yet, for all that's been written about the Net, there's been little consideration of how, exactly, it's reprogramming us. The Net's intellectual ethic remains obscure. The Net even changes the structure of other media from newspapers and magazines to television.[13]

Is our uniquely human gift of imagination threatened by today's over-abundance of images? Do our mass-produced and computer-generated images already imagine on our behalf? Is it reasonable to assume that even today's prevailing political pragmatism and lack of social visions and utopias are a consequence of a withering of political imagination? Are the expanding realms of fantasy life and daydream images a surrogate for genuine, individual and autonomous imagination and human affection? My anxious answer to all these questions is: yes.

Image production and the feasibility of architecture

In the era that preceded printing and mass reading, the cathedral with its sculptures, frescos and stained-glass windows was a seminal medium for conveying biblical texts and events to the largely illiterate congregation. The invention and deployment of printing made the book available to the masses and also became an incentive for the skill of reading.

Victor Hugo appended an enigmatic paragraph to the eighth edition of *Notre-Dame de Paris* (1831) entitled 'ceci tuera cela' ('this will kill that'), pronouncing the death sentence of architecture: 'In the fifteenth century [...] Human thought discovered a means of perpetuating itself in a more lasting and resistant form than architecture. It was simpler and easier as well. Architecture was dethroned. To Orpheus's stone letters succeeded Gutenberg's leaden type.'[14]

Hugo further examines this thought, which he places in the mouth of the Archdeacon of Notre-Dame: 'The foreshadowing that the human mind in changing its form would change its mode of expression, that the foremost idea of every generation would no longer be written on the same material, with the same manner; that the stone book, so solid and lasting, would give way to the paper book, still more solid and lasting.'[15]

Although Hugo's prophecy has been quoted time and again, its meaning for the course of architectural history has not, I think, been correctly interpreted. Hugo's prediction that architecture as the most important cultural medium would lose its status to newer media, has undoubtedly come true. But the new media have not ousted architecture because of their greater strength and durability, as Hugo predicted, but for exactly the opposite reasons: because they are fast, fleeting and dispensable. The printed book signified the first major step towards today's visual and simultaneous world. Early books on architecture, along with increasing travels – the Grand Tour – facilitated the propagation of stylistic ideals, such as the Palladian principles of architecture. At the same time that architectural ideals gained universality through their presence in the printed form, architecture lost its status as the most important locus of cultural information, in accordance with Hugo's prediction.

When even styles have become articles of conscious elaboration and consumption in today's consumer society, architecture has proved to be a hopelessly cumbersome medium of communication compared with the novel forms of disposable mass media. The fundamental meaning of architecture, even in the civilisation of the image, is integration and stability, as Sir Christopher Wren preached, but these qualities are in open conflict with the ideology of consumption. In fact, the normally long lifespan of buildings and other material constructions is in evident conflict with the ideas of momentary consumption, designed aging and repeated replacement. The strategy of consumerism requires ephemerality, alienation and the splintering of consciousness. A coherent view of the world would undoubtedly reveal the insanity of obsessive growth and consumption.

Architecture and the spectacle

Architecture has always fictionalised reality and culture through turning human settings into images and metaphors of idealised order and life, into fictionalised architectural narratives. Historically, architecture has also negotiated between the cosmic and human dimensions, eternity and present, gods and mortals. It has a central role in creating and projecting an idealised self-image of the given culture. This idealising objective is as clear in Greek architecture and polis (illustration, page 122, The Acropolis, Athens, Greece) as in Roman architectural structures and the organisation of the Roman city. A special realm of idealised architecture includes utopias and fictional architectural projects that were not even intended to be built, such as Giovanni Battista Piranesi's (1720–78) famous Carceri d'Invenzione drawings, the projects of the French utopists at the time of the French Revolution, and the visions of glass architecture of the German Expressionist architects. However, today's forceful imaging techniques and instantaneous architectural imagery often seem to create a world of autonomous architectural fictions, which totally neglect the fundamental existential soil and objectives of the art of building. This is an alienated architectural world without gravity and materiality, hapticity and compassion. The earlier visions of architecture reflected a viable form of culture and lifestyle whereas today's computer-generated visions usually appear as mere graphic exercises without a sense of real life. Today's thematised settings and fictitious architectural simulacra, such as shopping malls and urban squares, exemplify this loss of cultural sincerity and innocence. Are we today being manipulated by images of our own making? Yes, we are, and the ecstatic architectural images of our era of personal exhibitionism and narcissism conceal the fundamental and decisive issues of lifestyle, and value, and they blur the view of an ethical and biologically sound future.

From The Society of the Spectacle, promoted by Guy Debord,[16] we are swiftly turning into the society of surveillance and manipulation. The secret control of behaviour and individual life through images and technical devices already extends beyond the visual mode; multi-sensory marketing manipulates experiences, feelings and desires through sounds, tactile sensations, tastes and smells. In fact, today we are colonised through all our senses. Such notions as 'multisensory marketing', 'branding of the senses', 'sensory persuasion', 'tapping the sensorial subconscious', 'canalizing the mind-space', and 'hypersensuality of the contemporary market place' are used to describe these novel sensory strategies of scientifically informed marketing.[17] This expansion of sensory colonisation is exemplified by the recent attempt by the manufacturers of Harley-Davidson motorcycles to patent the characteristic coarse and masculine sound of their engine.[18]

A peculiar form of architectural 'colonisation' takes place through the uncritical application of technologies, such as efficient mechanical air-conditioning, which make it possible to build in the same universal style everywhere regardless of local climates.

Today's signature architecture seeks the same kind of close-circuit effect and product identification, and there are even examples of 'franchised' architecture, commercialised projects by the globalised offices of signature architects which aspire to express a recognisable brand. The great empires of the history of civilisations have always marked their territories by a specific architecture, and architecture has always promoted power. Today's globalised image-architecture aggressively claims the territory of the globalised market economy, the latest phase of worldwide capitalism.

Consumerism and its primary tool, publicity, even have ideological consequences. 'Publicity turns consumption into a substitute for democracy. The choice of what one eats (or wears or drives) takes the place of significant political choice. Publicity helps to mask and compensate for all that is undemocratic within society. And it also masks what is happening in the rest of the world', John Berger argued more than three decades ago.[19] Berger's argument suggests that we are living in a world of multiple realities and that we are forcefully exposed to make-believe realities. In today's world of instant global information and fluid capital, it is more evident than ever that an always expanding veil of disguise and mental conditioning frequently masks the realm of real intentions. It has become the hopeless task of critical journalism and various citizen movements to attempt to unmask the fabricated reality that we are forced to live in.

Images of control and emancipation

THE COMMANDING AND THE EMANCIPATING IMAGE

Images either focus and control the subject's attention and awareness for purposes of manipulating emotion and behaviour, or they liberate and inspire his/her imagination opening up a dimension of individual imaginative freedom.

Ludwig Hohlwein, *Und Du? (And You?)*, 1932. Political poster, offset lithograph, 117.5 × 80.6 cm.

The commanding image of a political poster. The image weakens the viewer's sense of self by focusing his/her imagination.

Sigurdur Gudmundsson, *Encore* (detail), 1991.

The emancipating poetic image of an Icelandic artist. The image empowers the viewer and opens up his/her imagination.

The notion 'image' is used frequently and fundamentally in differing meanings and varying contexts. The very same word is used indiscriminately for pictures, percepts, and entities of imagination, dream and daydream. Images are deployed for countless purposes, but there are two opposite types of images in relation to the individual freedom of the subject: images that dictate, manipulate and condition, and others that emancipate, empower and inspire. The first type is exemplified by images devised for political and consumer conditioning, the second by emancipatory poetic and artistic images. The first category narrows down, confines and weakens the freedom, choice and individuality of the subject by means of focusing and channelling his/her attention and awareness into a forced pattern, often grounded in the subject's sense of guilt and inferiority. The latter category of images opens up, fortifies and liberates by means of strengthening personal imagination, emotion and affect. The first category of images weakens us and makes us more uncertain of ourselves and dependent on authority, whereas poetic imagery reinforces our sense of self, autonomy and individual independence. The poetic images are images of individual integrity and freedom.

Altogether, images open up a direct channel to the human mind and emotion, and this channel can be used for multifarious and even opposite

purposes, humane or totalitarian, benevolent or cynical ends. Even in historiography, countless fragmented facts are compiled into images and narratives, and our understanding of history is fully dictated by these condensed and pre-narrated images of the fundamentally unfocused and shapeless temporal flow of places, personalities and events. The progression of history is normally told as a narrative between the milestones of wars, agreements, discoveries and great personalities; notoriously, standard histories are the stories of the winners.[20]

The development of imaging technologies and the mass production of fictitious narratives have already reversed the notions of reality and fiction. The merging of reality and fantasy, fact and fiction, ethical concerns and aesthetics, past and future, is one of the fundamental strategies in today's political and economic practices. Kearney sees the cultural situation critically indeed: 'We are at an impasse where the very rapport between *imagination* and *reality* seems not only inverted but subverted altogether.'[21] But the art world too is frequently an authoritatively pre-narrated and manipulated realm. The financial fact that entire nations today are living on credit is another alarming indication of the speeding up of life and the hold of fictitious realities; we are increasingly living in the future tense and losing the sense of the present.

Since time immemorial, the cultural task of storytelling, literature and art was to produce and maintain 'the other level of reality' – to use a notion of Herbert Marcuse[22] – that of dreams, beliefs, myths and ideals, for the purpose of creating an essential mental counterpoint to the mundane, and usually depressing, everyday experience of reality. During recent decades, however, the ethical responsibility of artists and writers seems to have reversed, and their task today is to strengthen our experience of the real. In the preface to his bestseller novel *Crash* (1973), JG Ballard argues to this effect, as he suggests that the relation of fiction and reality is in the process of turning upside down. We live increasingly in worlds of fiction and, therefore, the task of the writer is not any longer to invent fiction. Fictions are already here, and the 'writer's task is to invent reality'.[23]

The sense of the real

The condition of architecture has changed similarly. In a world which is increasingly fictionalised by an architecture of the commercialised image, and the enticing and seducing architecture of the retinal image, the task of the critical, profound and responsible architect is to create and defend the sense of the real. Instead of creating, or supporting a world of fantasy, the task of architecture is to strengthen our experience of the real in the spheres of perception and experience, as well as in cultural and social interaction. When our settings are turning into thematised and fabricated facades of fictitious culture – simulacra, to use a notion frequently used by Umberto Eco and other philosophers of post-modernity – the duty of responsible architecture is to defend the authenticity and autonomy of human experience. In the world of simulacra, simulation and virtuality, the ethical task of architects is to provide the touchstone of the real.

In my view, in the near future, the notion of the 'real' will increasingly imply what is justifiable in the biological perspective, both past and future. The notion of the real in our settings of life cannot be endlessly expanded and relativised; we are biological and historical beings whose entire physical, metabolic and neural systems have been optimally tuned to the reality of physical, ecological and biological facts. The human reality, as well as our future, is undeniably grounded in our biological and cultural past as much as in our wisdom concerning the future.

One of the basic reasons why the image has become such a forceful means of manipulation lies in the historical fact that logocentric Western philosophical, scientific as well as pedagogic thinking has neglected, or even entirely denied, the role of imagery and imagination in human thought, communication and everyday life. As a consequence, the image has been taken hostage from the realm of serious thinking and research, and it is being increasingly forcefully exploited for manipulative purposes. This is again paradoxical in a culture dominated by vision to the degree that vision has been accepted as the common metaphor for truth.[24]

There is no doubt about the fact that the humanity of the third millennium is a result of hundreds of thousands of years of human imagination and imagery. We are creatures of the life-world who have deliberately tamed and made ourselves. Images have served humanity in freeing us from the overpowering biological imperatives. But have we ourselves become victims of our own imagination? Has human imagination, combined with the desire for power and control, turned against ourselves as a biological species? Again, my answer to my questions is: yes, I believe so.

If imagination and images have emancipated the human race, couldn't the re-humanised image liberate us again? Couldn't the poetic and embodied image, the unselfish, disinterested and authentically curious imagination open up an optimistic future and emancipate us again?

This book was written with the belief that we can liberate and sensitise ourselves through a re-mythicised and re-poeticised understanding of the world, and that human imagination is autonomous, self-generative and limitless. It is encouraging that during the past few decades, scientific imagery seems to have approached poetic imagery, and vice versa. We live in an imaginative world – or worlds – of our own making, and the future of humanity rests entirely on our capacity for imagination. The following chapters analyse the essence of the mental image and imagination, and suggest ways in which we might go about re-rooting the art of architecture in its existential soil.

References

1 Richard Kearney, *The Wake of Imagination,* Routledge (London), 1994, p 3.
2 Italo Calvino, *Six Memos for the Next Millennium,* Vintage Books (New York), 1988, p 57.
3 Richard Kearney, *The Wake of Imagination,* 1994, p 383.
4 As quoted in Richard Kearney, *Poetics of Imagining: From Husserl to Lyotard,* Harper Collins Academic (London), 1991, p 8.
5 The study is referred to in Kearney, *The Wake of Imagination,* 1994, p 1.
6 As quoted in Norris Kelly Smith, 'Crisis in Jerusalem', *Late Entries,* Vol II, Rizzoli International Publications (New York), 1980, p 108.
7 Most notably, Fredric Jameson in *Postmodernism, or, The Cultural Logic of Late Capitalism,* Duke University Press (Durham), 1991, and David Harvey in *The Condition of Postmodernity,* Blackwell Publishers (Cambridge, MA and Oxford, UK), 1990.

'Everything tends to flatten out at the level of contemporaneity and simultaneity, thus producing a de-historisation of experience', Jameson asserts (p 9). Harvey points out the flattening of artistic thought: 'It is hardly surprising that the artist's relation to history […] has shifted, that in the era of mass television there has emerged an attachment to surfaces rather than roots, to collage rather than in-depth work, to superimposed quoted images rather than worked surfaces, to a collapsed sense of time and space rather than solidly achieved cultural artifact' (p 61).
8 Richard Kearney, *The Wake of Imagination,* 1994, p 2.
9 Ibid.
10 Ibid.
11 Ibid. p 6.
12 The most useful neurological studies for this context are listed in the Selected Bibliography on pp 140–143.
13 Nicholas Carr, 'Is Google Making Us Stupid?' (http://www.theatlantic.com/magazine/archive/2008/07/is-google-making-us-stupid/6868/).
14 Victor Hugo, *The Hunchback of Notre-Dame*, trans Catherine Liu, The Modern Library (New York), 2002, p 168. The unfortunate title of the English translation, which Hugo himself disliked, makes the deformed bellringer the protagonist instead of the cathedral itself.
15 Victor Hugo, *The Hunchback of Notre-Dame,* 2002, p 162.
16 Guy Debord, *The Society of the Spectacle,* Zone Books (New York), 1995.
17 David Howes, 'Hyperesthesia, or, The Sensual Logic of Late Capitalism', in *Empire of the Senses,* edited by David Howes, Berg Publishers (Oxford and New York), 2005, pp 281–303.
18 David Howes, *Empire of the Senses,* 2005, p 288.
19 John Berger, *The Ways of Seeing*, The British Broadcasting Corporation (London), 1977, p 149.
20 Jared Diamond's history of the human settlement of the world, *Guns, Germs, and Steel*, WW Norton & Company (New York and London), 1999, narrates the gradual distribution of the human species around the world from its origins in East Africa, following the logic of actual movements of groups of humans. His story reads as an entirely different causality in comparison with standard histories.
21 Richard Kearney, *The Wake of Imagination,* 1994, p 3.
22 Herbert Marcuse, *One-Dimensional Man: Studies in the Ideology of Advanced Industrial Society,* Beacon Press (Boston), 1964, p 57.
23 As quoted in Lars Fr H Svendsen, *Ikävystymisen filosofia* [*A Philosophy of Boredom*], Kustannusosakeyhtiö Tammi (Helsinki), 1999, p 92.
24 For the hegemony of vision and logocentric thinking, see my previous books *The Eyes of the Skin* (1995 and 2005) and *The Thinking Hand* (2009), as well as the numerous books referred to in these two studies.

2
Language, thought and image

Between concept and image there is no possibility of synthesis. Nor indeed of filiation.[1]

Gaston Bachelard, *Gaston Bachelard: On Poetic Imagination and Reverie*, 1998

The words of silent speech are not images; there are really no verbal images, for a word that has become an image is no longer a sign.[2]

Jean-Paul Sartre, *The Psychology of Imagination*, 1948

The relationships and interactions between imagery and language, perception and thought, are fundamental to the understanding of the human mind and creativity. In the past, the prevailing views of language neglected the role of images. During the last few decades, however, psychological and psycholinguistic experiments have revealed and proved the crucial role of mental images, or neural representations, in language and thought. These views have a crucial significance especially in the philosophies and methodologies of education.

WORDS AND VISUAL IMAGERY

The current assumption is that speech originates in gesture. The image has the capacity to communicate and transmit meaning without words and even beyond verbalised meanings.

Several of René Magritte's paintings point out the arbitrariness of words. 'The knowledge that the brain has about other things than its own storage system is stored by homeomorphic mental models' (Strømnes, 2006, p 31).

Image and language

The traditional Western attitude has stubbornly maintained the view that language and thinking are purely incorporeal and disembodied psychological phenomena. According to this attitude, there are tangible material things, on the one hand, and disembodied thought, on the other, and thinking is attached solely to our linguistic faculties.[3] This attitude prevails today even in established scholarly thinking, as exemplified by the recent argument of two esteemed linguistic scholars quoted by Frode J Strømnes in his book *The Fall of the Word and the Rise of the Mental Model,* which aspires to seize the word from its hegemonic position in the tradition of Western thought:

Jannis Kounellis, *Porta Murata (Walled Porch)*, 1990. Carbon, mouth of the artist.

The meaning of the visual image may often be impossible to express in words.

René Magritte, *Ceci n'est pas une pomme (This is not an apple)*, 1969. Private collection.

Magritte made several paintings on the discrepancy between words and images.

> Thoughts – or, as they are sometimes called, 'propositional attitudes' … are inner representations (and misrepresentations) of the external world … they must be language-like in character. First, thoughts seem to have the same semantic properties as sentences of human languages … Second, thoughts have the syntax of sentences … Finally, thoughts are like sentences in being abstract … Images, maps and diagrams may be *associated with* thoughts, particularly with perceptually based ones, but they are not themselves thoughts.

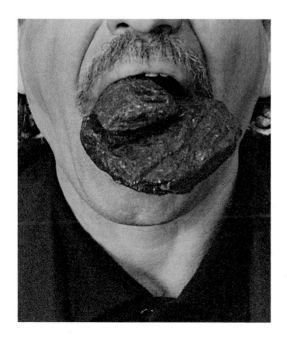

Depictive representation is too rich and ambiguous to capture the content
of thought … In sum, many thoughts are unpicturable; any picture could be
associated with many thoughts. Thought and talk are abstract, and abstract in
the same way. [Italics in the quote.][4]

We tend to believe that we think and communicate directly through words
and linguistic structures, when, in fact, we think and communicate through
mental images and models, or neural patterns. We keep constantly building,
comparing, storing and exchanging mental, or neural, models which are
mediated and elaborated through linguistic structures and words.

Recent psycholinguistic research has convincingly confirmed the use of
mental images and neural models in processes of thinking and speaking.
These research findings fully support the assumption that corporeal mental
models contain knowledge, and these are also used in various symbol systems.
According to psycholinguist Strømnes, there does not seem to exist any
empirical evidence to support: 'the view that non-analogue thoughts and
propositions have psychological reality, while there is very much support for
the view that analogue neural entities are essential to thinking and problem
solving'.[5] He makes a further clarification: 'Accordingly, one can maintain
that the neural correlates of words are merely addresses, which tell where
the neural entities carrying knowledge are stored in the brain. Thus, the
knowledge that the brain has about other things than its own storage system
is stored by *homeomorphic mental models*.'[6] Jean-Paul Sartre formulates the
idea of the mediating role of the word: 'As meaning, a word is but a beacon:
it presents itself, awakens a meaning, and this meaning never returns to the
word but goes out to the thing and the word is dropped.'[7]

In addition to the undeniable reality of imagery in thought and language, it
has also become evident that this imagery is grounded in embodiment, as
our mental imagery arises fundamentally from and refers to our body and
our existence in the 'flesh of the world'.[8] Maurice Merleau-Ponty's notions of
the flesh of the world and 'the Chiasm'[9] turn us into true participants in the
world instead of experiencing ourselves as mere observers. Verbalised thought
seems to be an articulation and termination of a fundamentally embodied
process or reaction. Language appears to articulate and express embodied
and neural energies and processes; speech does not arise from words but
the cognitive process of sensory and neural activation terminates in a verbal

expression. 'The body creates its sensations; therefore there is a corporeal imagination,' as the philosopher/psychoanalyst Cornelius Castoriadis claims.[10] As I begin to express an argument, I do not have the idea or sentence verbally formulated in my mind. I feel an embodied pressure to express something valid in relation to the situation at hand, and the words emerge to shape this embodied reaction. It is as if my body or my embodied existence, with its context and historicity of experience, were speaking through the mediation of my tongue. I speak as an ingredient of the flesh of the world, and speech is fundamentally an existential mode of communication in the same way as artistic expression.[11]

To explain the artistic means by which poets and novelists are able to make their readers construct complete and complex visual settings from printed words, philosopher/aesthetician Elaine Scarry poses a thought-provoking question in her book *Dreaming by the Book*: 'By what miracle is a writer able to incite us to bring forth mental images that resemble in their quality not our own daydreaming but our own [...] perceptual acts?'[12] In her view, great writers from Homer, Flaubert and Rilke to today's master writers, such as Seamus Heaney, have intuited, by means of words, how the brain perceives images. The suggestion that writers would intuitively imitate the perceptual processes of the brain and thus be able to expand the reader's visual imagination and, in a way, even direct his/her imagination, sounds far-fetched. However, Semir Zeki, one of the most authoritative neurobiologists, makes a surprisingly parallel suggestion in the case of visual art: '[I]n a large measure, the function of art and the function of the visual brain are one and the same, or at least [that] the aims of art constitute an extension of the functions of the brain'.[13] He confesses: '[...] I hold the somewhat unusual view that artists are in some sense neurologists, studying the brain with techniques that are unique to them, but studying unknowingly the brain and its organization nevertheless'.[14] Artists expand our visual imagination by intensifying the excitation of specific areas in our visual brain. In Zeki's view, great artists intensify the imagination of the beholder by intuitively imitating the manner in which the visual cortex constructs images. Zeki's views are not mere theoretical speculation as they are based on his rigorous studies of the neural processes in the visual brain.

On the basis of his studies on Johannes Vermeer, Zeki proposes that in a work of art an interplay of constancy and ambiguity both excites and expands the

INCOMPLETENESS AND
AMBIGUITY IN ART

Incompleteness and
ambiguity of the artistic
image activate our minds
and maintain an active
attention and interest. Semir
Zeki points out that artistic
ambiguity is not vagueness
or uncertainty in the usual
sense of these words, 'but on
the contrary, certainty – the
certainty of many different,
and essential, conditions,
each of which is equal to
the others, all expressed in
a single profound painting,
profound because it is so
faithfully representative of so
much' (Zeki, 1999, p 26).

Michelangelo, *Awakening
Slave*, h. 267 cm, c 1519.
Galleria dell'Accademia,
Florence.

The sculptor executed a
number of 'incomplete'
works in which matter and
image are set in an eternal
battle.

Jan Vermeer, *The Art of
Painting*, c. 1666–67. Oil
on canvas, 120 × 100 cm.
Kunsthistorisches Museum,
Vienna.

Vermeer's paintings are
extremely precise in their
visual rendering of the scene
but the human narrative
offers numerous open-ended
interpretations.

imagination. In the case of Vermeer's paintings, his visual imagery projects a high degree of constancy, whereas the depicted human relations of the visually suggested narratives remain highly enigmatic. This suggestion also seems to explain why incomplete or 'formless' images have such a stimulating effect on our imagination. Michelangelo's 'incomplete' sculptures, such as his muscular slaves struggling to liberate their images of flesh from their imprisonment in stone, seem to exploit Zeki's neurological principle.[15]

The recent findings of empirical research and philosophical investigations oblige us to alter the accepted views of language itself. Yet, there seems to be a strong cultural resistance to question our deep-rooted assumptions about the world, the role of language in cognition, as well as ourselves as cognitive and imagining beings.

The biblical claim of the primacy of the word – the Genesis in the Gospel of John reads: 'In the Beginning was the Word, and the Word was with God, and the Word was God' (Jn 1:1), and continues: 'and the Word became flesh' (Jn 1:14) – seems to have made us blind to the role and power of the image.[16] There is not much doubt about the ontological precedence: the image emerged first. The image gave rise to embodied gesture, and then the gesture was transformed to language articulated by vocal cords and, finally, by characters on paper.

The philosophical image

The hegemonic line of Western philosophy has also generally undervalued the significance of the imagination and image, or it has even entirely neglected these mental realities. As philosopher Edward S Casey argues: 'Preoccupied by logocentric concerns, philosophers have been consistently sceptical of imagining and its products. Their scepticism stems largely from a conception of philosophical thinking as image-free.'[17] Already at the beginning of last century, Francis Galton made the same observation as he argued:

> A habit of suppressing mental imagery must [therefore] characterize men who deal with abstract ideas; and as their power of dealing easily and firmly with these ideas is the surest criterion of a high order of intellect, we should expect that the visualizing faculty would be starved by disuse among philosophers, and this is precisely what I found in inquiry to be the case.[18]

Casey argues further:

> Ever since Plato [Plato placed imagination in the lowest rank of mental faculties], philosophers have condemned recourse to imagery as an inferior form of mental activity – as at best a crutch for, and at worst a debasement of, pure reflection. Philosophical thinking, proclaims Martin Heidegger, is 'charmless and image-poor'. It remains moot, however, whether there is or can be such a thing as strictly imageless thinking, a thinking that dispenses with images altogether, to become 'thought thinking itself', in Aristotle's provocative and revealing phrase.[19]

Regardless of this strong tradition to disparage the image and imagination as true and operative ingredients of human consciousness, thought and memory, it has gradually become evident that these faculties constitute the very ground of humanity itself. It is impossible to explain the marvellous human faculties of grasping, remembering and understanding vast entities of information – such as one's own persona, with its entire historicity, or the continuum of time and places through one's life – without the existence of embodied schemes, images, mental models and embodied metaphors that structure, organise, integrate and maintain huge volumes of fragmented sense and memory data. It is equally impossible to think of an individual or collective ethical responsibility without the capacity for imagination that is capable of projecting and concretising the consequences of alternative behavioural choices.

Several philosophers of the phenomenological orientation, such as Jean-Paul Sartre, Gaston Bachelard, Edward S Casey and Richard Kearney, have developed convincing philosophies of the image and imagination. These philosophies serve today as the ground for the understanding of human mental activities and imagination as well as creative capacities. These philosophical views also decisively illuminate the phenomena of the arts and architecture that often tend to appear irrational or mystical.

The historical suppression of imagery in the prevailing theories of thinking notwithstanding, the acknowledgement of the image and imagination is not entirely new, as Aristotle had already made the significant remark: 'The soul never thinks without an image.'[20] Aristotle's observation inevitably brings to mind Wittgenstein's assumptions, more than two millennia later, 'A proposition is a picture of reality' (4.021), and, 'A proposition states something only in so far as it is a picture' (4.03).[21]

The meanings of image and imagination

The word 'image' is commonly used as a synonym for 'picture', 'visual depiction' or even 'photograph'. Words, such as 'image', 'to image', 'to imagine', 'imagery', 'imagination', 'imaginative', 'imaginal', 'imaginary', 'mental image', 'primal image', 'affective image' – not to mention numerous related notions such as, 'fantasy', 'metaphor', 'metonymy', 'icon', 'archetype' – form a host of poorly defined and loosely used concepts and words. Our common understanding of the notions of 'imagination' and 'image' is very vague indeed. This lack of definition and focus has its distinct role in our weak grasp of sensory and mental phenomena in general. Altogether, our culture has a poor understanding and tolerance for intrinsically diffuse, highly autonomous, variable and indeterminate phenomena, such as human emotion, or mental imagery and imagination.

This is also one of the reasons why our innately diffuse and vague creative capacities and acts are also poorly and conflictingly understood. The image has been traditionally acknowledged in its perceptual, mimetic and mnemonic roles, but less as a medium of thought, creative exploration and artistic expression. The notion has been frequently applied in areas of public relations and business ('public image', 'corporate image'), and pictorial arts, but much less in literature or architecture. The recent emergence of the 'pictorial' architecture of an eye-catching image has, however, introduced the notion to architectural contexts. The fact that we also deploy the notions of 'hypnagogic', 'dream' and 'hallucinatory' images – all of which have often been regarded as pathological or irresponsible – has further confused the understanding and acceptance of imagery as a central vehicle of our healthy and productive mental processes, consciousness and creative capacity.

The most common confusion occurs between sensory percepts and imaginative mental images. In his book *The Psychology of Imagination*, Jean-Paul Sartre maintains that, 'imagining is to be distinguished from perceiving not by reference to the objects it intends, but by reference to the act of intending. The mental image is not just a thing existing alongside other things, it is a unique *orientation* of consciousness towards things' (Sartre's italics).[22] 'The two worlds, real and imaginary, are composed of the same objects, only the grouping and interpretation of these objects varies. What defines the imaginary world and also the world of the real, is an attitude of consciousness', Sartre writes.[23]

> The image and the percept are not therefore different objects of consciousness; they are different ways of being conscious of objects. The image is the relation of consciousness to the object; in other words, it means a certain manner in which the object makes its appearance to consciousness, or if one prefers, a certain manner in which consciousness presents an object to itself.[24]

In Sartre's way of thinking, the worlds of perception and imagination are mutually exclusive, although they may deal with the same objects and aspects of the world. Wittgenstein also points out the exclusivity of the two acts: 'While I am looking at an object, I cannot imagine it.'[25] The recent research findings showing that percepts and mental images take place in the very same areas of the brain do not seem to invalidate the philosophers' claim.

Regardless of the historically prevailing view of imageless and essentially verbal thought, seminal theories of purely visual thinking, such as those of Paul Klee, Wassily Kandinsky, Gyorgy Kepes and Rudolf Arnheim, have decisively expanded the understanding of the realm of thought and creativity.[26] Thinking and articulating expression and emotion through music and dance are, also, clearly outside the verbal realm and engaged with our senses of hearing, movement and proprioception.[27] However, these practical and theoretical propositions arising from artistic perception and experience have been met with suspicion and resistance in wider philosophical circles, regardless of their evident validity in the realms of art and artistic education. Also, statements of great scientists on their creative thought processes, such as Albert Einstein's description of the role of visual and muscular aspects in his mathematical and physical thought, have been bypassed as mere curiosities.[28]

It is especially regrettable that prevailing general educational philosophies around the Western world have grossly undervalued the role of imagery and imagination as well as the sensory and embodied dimensions of human existence and thought. This bias is reflected in the fact that art and architectural education as well as thesis works in these areas most often have to be validated by 'academic standards', which rather categorically mean the usual empirical and logocentrically theoretised criteria, instead of being encountered and assessed through their inherent criteria of sensory impact, artistic imagery and emotional content. Yet, it is beyond doubt that all our sensory, metabolic and neural systems 'think' in the sense of gathering and handling information of life situations, and projecting and initiating meaningful reactions. We need to say even more; as the studies of Mark Johnson, philosopher, and George Lakoff, linguist, suggest, thinking itself is fundamentally an embodied act, and our entire neural system participates in these processes.[29] Neurological research has 'placed' distinct activities in the brain, but there is convincing evidence that thinking is 'placeless' and relational.

'The painter "takes his body with him" says [Paul] Valéry. Indeed we cannot imagine how a *mind* could paint,' Merleau-Ponty argues.[30] It is even more unthinkable that a mind, detached from embodiment, could conceive architecture because of the indisputable role of the body in the very constitution of architecture; architecture takes place in the flesh of the world and in the carnal and lived human reality. With the exception of the deformed and disturbed mind, and certain pathological hallucinations, human thoughts take place in the same flesh of the world which is also occupied by our bodily being. Thus, thinking is not primarily abstract or alienated from lived reality; it articulates, compresses, distils and amalgamates live experiences. As Jean-Paul Sartre argues: '[U]nderstanding is not a quality coming to human reality from the outside; it is its characteristic way of existing.'[31] The processes of thought are fundamentally open-ended in the way that life processes in general are open-ended and self-regulating.

The pioneering American psychologist William James had already made a significant remark on this fundamental dynamism, relatedness and historicity of thought, in 1890: 'Every definite image in the mind is steeped and dyed in the free water that flows around it. With it goes the sense of its relations, near and remote, the dying echo of whence it came to us, the dawning sense of whither it is to lead. The significance, the value of the image, is all in this halo or penumbra that surrounds and escorts it.'[32]

At the beginning of last century, Ezra Pound, the 'Imagist' poet, called for the 'shock and stroke' of new poetry, based on the image, to liberate poetic imagination from its tired logocentric mannerisms.[33] In my view, architecture, also, calls for the same 'shock and stroke' of true lived life and authentic experience in order to recover the ground of architectural reality.

The nature of imagination

The imagination is one of the highest prerogatives of man. By this faculty he unites former images and ideas, independently of the will, and thus creates brilliant and novel results ... The dream is an involuntary [kind] of poetry.[34]

Charles Darwin

The mind is at every stage a theatre of simultaneous possibilities.[35]

William James

The act of imagination [...] is a magical act. It is an incantation destined to make the object of one's thought, the thing one desires, appear in such a way that one can take possession of it.[36]

Jean-Paul Sartre

In our prevailing naive realism, we believe that our consciousness is primarily engaged in an objectively given and collectively shared world. Yet, even a momentary critical introspection reveals that, 'Artists or not, we are irrepressible imaginers in everyday life, where we indulge in imaginative activity persistently and not merely as an occasional *divertissement*.'[37] We process and project meaningful reactions (thoughts) through our entire constitution. We need to acknowledge that we live in mental and fundamentally subjective worlds of memory, dream and imagination as much as in a perceived material, physical and experientially shared world. Paradoxically, our world is given to us, but at the same time, it is of our own making. In short, we encounter the world as images, and this imagery is highly autonomous; it does not advance through causation but through the whimsical paths of the unconscious and the unpredictable ways of association.

Imagination is often regarded as a mere diversion of consciousness, such as the derogatory connotation of daydreaming, or as a mental prerequisite for creativity, but we actually live in a continuous dialogue between imagination and 'reality', the mental and the physical. As Edward Casey points out, 'in certain situations, it is even more difficult not to imagine than to imagine in the first place'.[38] The philosopher also argues that, 'there is no way to distinguish imagination *in kind* from other mental acts, all of which also stem from sensory experience […] The world of a poem, therefore, does not differ in kind from the world of memory: all differences are differences of degree'.[39]

There is an unexpected neurological affinity between images and percepts. Recent research shows that images take place in the same zones of the brain as visual perceptions, and that the first are experientially equally as real as the latter; the regions of the brain which participate in the formation of images are the same as those in which the neural signals from the eyes, giving rise to visual perceptions, are initially processed. The neural activity in the area of the visual cortex related with images is similar to the activity of looking at real pictures.[40] However, when acknowledging the experiential affinity of perceived and imagined images, their ontological difference has to be firmly identified. In Gaston Barchelard's view: 'Imagination allows us to leave the ordinary course of things. Perceiving and imagining are as antithetical as presence and absence.'[41]

The faculty of imagination has been recognised and valued among writers, poets and other artists, as well as scientists of all times. Anatole France even gives imagination a higher status than knowledge: 'To know is nothing at all; to imagine is everything,'[42] whereas Charles Baudelaire regards imagination as the very source of our world: 'Imagination created the world.'[43]

The image has a multitude of faces. In order to understand how our own mind works and why we attach such strong affects to images, we need to analyse what really happens in our mind when we confront an artistic image, and embody it, or when we just simply imagine.

References

1 *Gaston Bachelard, On Poetic Imagination and Reverie*, selected, translated and introduced by Colette Gaudin, Spring Publications (Dallas, TX), 1998, p 5.
2 Jean-Paul Sartre, *The Psychology of Imagination*, Citadel Press (Secaucus, NJ), 1948, p 121.
3 Frode J Strømnes, *The Fall of the Word and the Rise of the Mental Model*, Peter Lang (Frankfurt am Main), 2006, p 19.
4 M Devitt and K Sterelny, *Language and Reality. An Introduction to the Philosophy of Language*, Blackwell (Oxford), 1987, pp 115–17, as quoted in Strømnes, *The Fall of the Word and the Rise of the Mental Model*, 2006, p 26.
5 Strømnes, *The Fall of the Word and the Rise of the Mental Model*, 2006, p 31.
6 Ibid.
7 Sartre, *The Psychology of Imagination*, 1948, p 30.
8 Maurice Merleau-Ponty describes the notion of the flesh in his essay 'The Intertwining – The Chiasm', in *The Visible and the Invisible*, Claude Lefort, editor, Northwestern University Press (Evanston, IL), 1969, fourth printing, 1992, pp 130–55.
9 Maurice Merleau-Ponty, *The Visible and the Invisible*, 1992.
10 As quoted in Arnold H Modell, *Imagination and the Meaningful Brain*, MIT Press (Cambridge, MA, and London, UK), 2006, p 69.
11 In his recent study of the consequences of embodiment in the human mind, *How the Body Shapes the Mind*, Shaun Gallagher makes a similar assumption about the origins of language: 'To the degree that embodiment shapes language,

one could conceive of the translation of embodied spatial frameworks into linguistic form, through the medium of gesture [...] One could imagine gesture as the origin of language, and spoken language gradually emerging from embodied movement, a special kind of oral motility. Speech on this view would be a sophisticated movement of the body. If there is some truth to this, it is not the complete truth. In addition, one needs to understand how gesture comes about, and whether it is generated out of instrumental or locomotive movement.' Shaun Gallagher, *How the Body Shapes the Mind*, Clarendon Press (Oxford), 2006, p 107.

For the origination of language in gesture, see: David F Armstrong, William C Stokoe and Sherman E Wilcox, *Gesture and the Nature of Language*, Cambridge University Press (Cambridge), 1995.
12 Elaine Scarry, *Dreaming by the Book*, Princeton University Press (Princeton, NJ), 2001, p 7.
13 Semir Zeki, *Inner Vision: An Exploration of Art and the Brain*, Oxford University Press (Oxford), 1999, p 1.
14 Ibid. p 10.
15 Ibid. pp 22–36.
16 Sigurd Bergmann, Professor of Religious Studies, actually argues for the primacy of the image: 'In the beginning was not the Word, contrary to the Gospel of John. In the beginning, however, was the icon, creation, expression, the visual inner experience, the order in chaos.' Bergmann asks: 'Are we suffering from a cultural deformation because of the written word's historically superior role in our minds and

thoughts? Can visual arts, both its creative and reflective aspect, rectify this deformation and perhaps abolish it?' Sigurd Bergmann, *In the Beginning is the Icon: A Liberative Theology of Images, Visual Arts and Culture*, Equinox (London and Oakville, CT), 2009, p 2.
17 Edward S Casey, *Imagining: A Phenomenological Study*, Indiana University Press (Bloomington and London), 1976, p X.
18 As quoted in Casey, *Imagining*, 1976, p X.
19 Casey, *Imagining*, 1976, p X.
20 Ibid. p 16. The quote derives from Aristotle, *De Anima*, 431a16.
21 Ludwig Wittgenstein, *Tractatus Logico-Philosophicus* (1918), Lightning Source (Milton Keynes), 2009, pp 33 and 34.
22 As quoted in Richard Kearney, *Poetics of Imagining: From Husserl to Lyotard*, Harper Collins Academic (London), 1991, p 49.
23 Jean-Paul Sartre, *The Psychology of Imagination*, 1948, p 27.
24 Ibid. p 8.
25 Ludwig Wittgenstein, *Zettel*, section 621, as quoted in Casey, *Imagining*, 1976, p 146.
26 See, for instance, Paul Klee, *The Thinking Eye*, G Wittenborn (New York); second edition, 1964, and *Pedagogical Sketchbook*, Faber and Faber (London), 1925; Wassily Kandinsky, *Point and Line to Plane*, Solomon R Guggenheim Foundation (New York), 1947; Gyorgy Kepes, *Language of Vision*, Paul Theobald (Chicago), 1961; Rudolf Arnheim, *Visual Thinking*, University of California (Berkeley and Los Angeles), 1969.

27 For the eye–mind–hand connection in architecture, crafts and artistic work, see Juhani Pallasmaa, *The Thinking Hand: Existential and Embodied Wisdom in Architecture*, John Wiley & Sons (London), 2009.
28 Einstein's letter published as Appendix II in Jacques Hadamard, *The Psychology of Invention in the Mathematical Field*, Princeton University Press (Princeton, NJ), 1949, pp 142–3.
29 George Lakoff and Mark Johnson, *Philosophy in the Flesh: The Embodied Mind and its Challenge to Western Thought*, Basic Books (New York), 1999.
30 Maurice Merleau-Ponty, *The Primacy of Perception*, Northwestern University Press (Evanston, IL), 1964, p 162.
31 Jean-Paul Sartre, *The Emotions: An Outline of a Theory*, Carol Publishing Group (New York), 1993, p 9.
32 William James, *The Principles of Psychology* (1890), Dover Publications (New York), 1950.
33 As referred to in JD McClatchy, 'Introduction', *Poets on Painters*, edited by JD McClatchy, University of California Press (Berkeley, Los Angeles, London), 1988, p XI.
34 As quoted in Modell, *Imagination and the Meaningful Brain*, 2006, p 25.
35 William James, *The Principles of Psychology*, Dover (New York), 1950, I, p 290.
36 Jean-Paul Sartre, *The Imaginary*, Routledge (London and New York), 2010, p 125.
37 Casey, *Imagining*, 1976, p 3.
38 Ibid. p 4.
39 Ibid. p 11.
40 Ilpo Kojo, 'Mielikuvat ovat aivoille todellisia' ['Images are real for the brain'], *Helsingin Sanomat*, Helsinki, 16.3.1996.
41 Gaston Bachelard, *Air and Dreams: An Essay On the Imagination of Movement*, Dallas Institute Publications (Dallas, TX), 1988, p 3.
42 As quoted in Casey, *Imagining*, 1976, p XI. Source of quote Anatole France, *The Crime of Sylvester Bonnard*, Harper (New York), 1890, Part II, Chapter 2.
43 As quoted in Casey, *Imagining*, 1976, p 1, source of quote Charles Baudelaire, 'La Reine des Facultés' in *Curiosités esthétiques [et] L'Art romantique*, Garnier (Paris), 1962, p 321.

3
The many faces of the image

When I speak of poetry, I am not thinking of it as a genre. Poetry is an awareness of the world, a particular way of relating to reality.[1]

Andrei Tarkovsky, *Sculpting in Time – Reflections on the Cinema*, 1986

[A true poem is one in which] the hairs stand on end, the eyes water, the throat is constricted, the skin crawls and a shiver runs down the spine.[2]

Robert Graves, *The White Goddess*, 1948

The notion of the image is commonly attached to a schematised visual representation or picture. Yet, in our mental life, we constantly deploy mental or imaginary images. The crucial faculty of the image is its magical capacity to mediate between physical and mental, perceptual and imaginary, factual and affectual. Poetic images, especially, are embodied and lived as part of our existential world and sense of self. Images, archetypes and metaphors structure our perceptions, thoughts and feelings, and they are capable of communicating messages of deep time as well as mediating epic narratives of human life and destiny.

The lived and embodied image

Poetry is a metaphysics of the moment. It has to convey within the space of
a short poem a vision of the universe and the secrets of a heart, a person,
things – and do so all at once. If it merely obeys the time scale of life, it is
something less than life; it can only be greater than life by immobilizing life
and experiencing on the spot, as it were, the dialectics of joy and pain. It is the
principle of an essential simultaneity in which the most scattered and disunited
being achieves unity.[3]

Gaston Bachelard, *The Right to Dream,* 1988

In the common use of language, the concept 'image' refers to a real sensory
percept, pictorial representation or an imaginative mental image. Differing
from the usual understanding of the word, the poetic image refers to an
evocative, affective and meaningful sensory experience that is layered,
associative and dynamic, and in constant interaction with memory and desire.
Echoing the Tarkovsky credo above, I do not refer to poetry as a genre of
artistic expression, but as the artistic sensibility in general. Thus the word
'poetic' in this book refers to subtle and visionary architectural ideas as well
as ideas in verse. Poetic images are mental frames that direct our associations,
emotions, reactions and thoughts. Due to its contradictory and often illogical
ingredients, the poetic image escapes rational, linear and exclusive reading and
explanation. It entices our senses, imagination and emotions, frequently it also
evokes our sense of empathy and compassion. It occupies our mind, conditions
our thoughts and feelings, and gives rise to an imaginative reality. The poetic
image transcends its material and rational essence.

The imaginative poetic realm arises at the encounter of the poetic image. Jorge
Luis Borges points out how this poetic reality emerges: 'The taste of the apple
[…] lies in the contact of the fruit with the palate, not in the fruit itself; in a
similar way […] poetry lies in the meeting of poem and reader, not in the lines
of symbols printed on the pages of a book. What is essential is the aesthetic
act, the thrill, the almost physical emotion that comes with each reading.'[4]

The poetic image of artistic expression is encountered in a fully embodied and
emotive manner in the flesh of the world. It is not a mere retinal or auditive
picture, or figure of representation or language, outside our personal and
lived domains. The poetic image is an internalised experience. With her notion
'projective identification', Melanie Klein suggests that we project fragments

of ourselves on to the other.[5] A similar projective identification seems to occur when we are experiencing a poetic image. We share our sense of life with our mental imagery; poeticised images seem to possess a life force of their own, like live creatures. Entering a space, for instance, implies an instant, unconscious exchange; I enter and occupy the space, and the space enters and occupies me. Also non-visual images become equally integral parts of the encounter in an embodied manner. The poeticised visual, auditory, haptic, olfactory and gustatory images are all experiential 'creatures' of our life-world.

Not only the material images of painting and sculpture, but also the language of poetry and literary fiction has its embodied character. Powerful words and literary expressions possess their spatiality, gravity and tactility – or solidity, as Elaine Scarry claims.[6] They project their own materiality and experiential cosmos. 'In order to achieve the "vivacity" of the material world, the verbal arts must somehow also imitate its "persistence" and, most crucially, its quality of "givenness". It seems almost certainly the case that it is the "instructional" character of the verbal arts that fulfils this mimetic requirement for "givenness".'[7] The Czech writer Bohumil Hrabal describes vividly the embodiment that takes place in the act of reading: 'When I read, I don't really read: I pop up a beautiful sentence in my mouth and suck it like a fruit drop or I sip it like a liqueur until the thought dissolves in me like alcohol. Infusing my brain and heart and coursing on through the veins to the root of each blood vessel.'[8]

Works of art, literature and architecture originate in the body of the maker and they return back to the body through the experience of the beholder/listener/reader of the work, or the dweller of the house, through the mediation of the artistic image. Charles Tomlinson, the poet, points out this bodily involvement in painting and poetry, both in the acts of making and re-experiencing the work: 'Painting wakes up the hand, draws-in your sense of muscular coordination, your sense of the body, if you like. Poetry also, as it pivots on its stresses, as it rides forward over the line endings, or comes to rest at pauses in the line, poetry also brings the whole man into play and his bodily sense of himself.'[9]

In his essay 'Eye and Mind', Merleau-Ponty makes a significant remark on embodiment in the art of painting: 'Quality, light, colour, depth, which are there before us, are there only because they awaken an echo in our body and because the body welcomes them [...] Things have an internal equivalence in me; they arouse in me a carnal formula of their presence.'[10]

SUBCONSCIOUS INTERPRETATIONS INFILTRATE PERCEPTION

It is characteristic of our perceptual system that we continuously scan the perceptual field for potential meaning. As, for example, Anton Ehrenzweig has argued, our sensory systems operate on conscious and unconscious levels, and seminal aspects of artistic imagery arise directly from the unconscious level. We also tend to see recognisable images and meanings in unintentional and accidental patterns, such as images of erosion.

Henri Michaux, Untitled, 1960. Museum of Modern Art, New York. Ink on paper, 29³/₈' × 42¹/₂' (74.5 × 107.8 cm). Gift of Michel Warren and Daniel Cordier.

The accidental configurations are given a vivid interpretive life by our imagination and unconscious.

Ryoan-ji kare-sansui Garden, The Temple of the Peaceful Dragon, Kyoto, c 1488.

The extremely simple configuration of 15 stones on a rectangle of raked sand is turned into imaginary landscapes of monumental scale by our imagination.

This 'carnal formula' gives the work of art its very sense of life. No doubt, musical experiences evoke similarly images and experiences of space, movement, density, duration, scale, progression, temperature and bodily tensions. Buildings address our body and sense of bodily balance, tension, proprioception and movement. Indeed, architectural spaces embrace and house our bodies. The architectural image is fundamentally an invitation for action; for instance, the floor invites movement and activity, the door is an invitation to enter or exit, the window to look out, the table to gather around.

Through history, architecture has been a means of mediating between the measureless cosmos and the scale of man, between divinities and mortals. At the same time, architectural spaces, dimensions and details echo and accommodate measures, movements and ergonomic characteristics of the human body in countless ways. A meaningful building establishes a dialogue between itself and the occupant's body as well as his/her memory and mind. We can surely conclude that the art form of architecture is fundamentally relational and dialectical in its very essence.

It is reasonable to speculate that our automatic and unconscious tendency to experience images as parts of our life-world has a bio-historical justification. Perceiving meaningless and unrelated images, detached from their essential contextual settings that give percepts their meaning in terms of survival, would not have given any evolutionary advantage. Meaninglessness and abstraction are not characteristics of the biological life-world. On the contrary, we are capable of grasping images in their complex completeness in an instant. In fact, we grasp the entity, the 'anatomy' and the meaning of an image before we are able to identify its details, or understand it intellectually. We tend to grasp every image, even the most vague and diffuse one, in its 'creature-like' life force, overall structure and significance. We seek meaning automatically even in arbitrary and meaningless images, such as accidental ink blots, or the 'formless' paintings of Henri Michaux (illustration, page 43, Henri Michaux, *Untitled*), the poet-painter, the painted muscular gestures and movement patterns of action painters, or the pattern of stones on raked sand in a dry Zen garden (illustration, page 43, Ryoan-ji kare-sansui Garden, The Temple of the Peaceful Dragon).

We experience these accidental and 'shapeless' visual formations as depictions of phenomena of the real world and life. The completeness and integrity of an image – whether literary, painterly, sculptural, musical or architectural – seems to arise from this subliminal perception and understanding of its 'organic' coherence and 'biological' essence. In my view, it is important to acknowledge that our systems of perception, sensing, comprehension and reaction evolved and tuned up for the purposes of survival in specific contexts tens of millions of years before deliberately fabricated images and gestures became a means of human communication, or of intentional emotional or artistic expression. This fundamental historicity of images, as well as our system of perceiving and grasping them, is usually overlooked.

Several scholars have recently studied the bio-historical ground of human preference for distinct types of landscapes and settings (reminiscent of the savannah condition in an early phase of human evolution), and the spatial situations that we generally judge safe and comfortable. The preferred spatial situation combines a sense of protectiveness of the immediate setting (refuge) with a wide vista of the environment providing a sense of control (prospect). Grant Hildebrand interestingly applies the refuge-prospect concept to the popularity of Frank Lloyd Wright's house designs, and shows that the master architect intuitively understood these deep reactions arising from our biocultural history. The sensory and mental appeal of fire surely reflects similar deep and primordial experiences of pleasure.[11]

Images have had their own lives for millions of years, and they have become fully integrated with the human life–world and system of reactions. Besides, there is no meaningless percept or image in the biological world as perceptions are related to existence and survival and, consequently, always have potential meaning and significance. Recent neurological studies, such as Semir Zeki's *Inner Vision: An Exploration of Art and the Brain* and John Onian's *Neuroarthistory*,[12] connect artistic phenomena with our neural and

THE LIFE FORCE OF THE ARTISTIC IMAGE

Profound artistic images possess their own life force. Through the process of imaginative projection we create a world, a universe, around them, and at the same time, we accept them as objects of our own life world. Our own experience and understanding of 'reality' keeps projecting new aspects and qualities on these magical images. Artistic images are timeless as we ourselves keep breathing life and movement into them.

Chinese Horse Palaeolithic Cave Painting at Lascaux, c 15,000–13,000 BCE.

The experiential and emotive reality of every art work is created anew at each encounter of the work. All art works are timeless as their experiential encounter always takes place in the present tense. The most ancient work approaches us with the same rigour as the most recent.

Constantin Brancusi, *Bird in Space*, 1940. Bronze. Musée National d'Art Moderne, Centre Pompidou, Paris, France.

Brancusi's images of birds, fish and seals project a surprising sense of life, 'the breath of life', in the words of the sculptor himself.

brain activities. As was suggested earlier, profound artistic talents seem to be capable of intuitively grasping fundamental aspects of the ways our brain and neural systems operate.

'Art must give suddenly, all at once, the shock of life, the sensation of breathing,' Constantin Brancusi exclaimed.[13] This is exactly the vivid quality and sense of life of the cave paintings, (illustration, above left) as well as Brancusi's own sculpted images of living creatures (illustration, above right). Regardless of their utmost formal reduction and condensation, his birds, fishes and human figures breathe life and suggest imaginative movement. Their abstraction is not lifeless stylisation or reduction, but a condensation of the very life force of the subject.

Every ingredient of an artistic image is injected with life. Charles Tomlinson describes the live, organicist quality of shadows in a painterly depiction of skulls:

> Shadow explores them. It sockets the eye-holes with black. It reaches like
> fingers into the places one cannot see. Skulls are a keen instance of this duality
> of the visible: it borders what the eye cannot make out, it transcends itself with

the suggestion of all that is there beside what lies within the eyes' possession: it
cannot be possessed.[14]

Gaston Bachelard suggests that poetic imagination, or 'poetic chemistry', as
he describes it, is closely related to pre-scientific thinking and an animistic
understanding of the world. In *The Philosophy of No: A Philosophy of the New
Scientific Mind* (1940), he describes the historical development of scientific
thought as a set of progressively more rationalised transitions from animism
through realism, positivism, rationalism and complex rationalism, to dialectical
rationalism.[15] 'The philosophical evolution of a special piece of scientific
knowledge is a movement through all these doctrines in the order indicated,'
Bachelard argues.[16] He holds that artistic thinking proceeds in the opposite
direction back towards a mythical and animistic understanding of the world.

Indeed, artistic expression is always essentially an animistic expression. There is
always more to the artistic image than the eye – or ear, nose, skin, tongue or
comprehension – can identify and reveal, because it is experienced as part of
the limitless domain of the real. Reality itself enriches and completes the poetic
image. More precisely, the artistic image projects its own imaginary life-world,
which is fused with our own sense of existence and life.

Images of matter

Matter is the unconscious of form [...] Only matter can become charged with
multiple impressions and feelings.[17]

Gaston Bachelard, *Water and Dreams*, 1999

Matter is a link. It has the effect of making unity. All art forms are based on
matter; they have to confront materiality [...] The word, the spoken or written
word, has the most immediate impact on human beings; in contrast, matter
speaks more slowly.[18]

Alvar Aalto, *Alvar Aalto, Synopsis*, 1970

Gaston Bachelard, the philosopher of the imagination and poetic image, wrote
a phenomenological study on each one of the four pre-Socratic elements –
earth, water, air and fire – in fact, he wrote two books on fire. He called these
elements 'hormones of the imagination'.[19] In the introduction 'Imagination

Modern art and architecture have usually aspired to the Albertian ideal of completion and perfection of form, 'to which nothing can be added or from which nothing can be subtracted'. Yet, incompleteness, erosion and destruction often give rise to exceptionally enticing and rich imageries that are images of matter itself. In John Ruskin's view: 'Imperfection is in some sort essential to all that we know of life. It is the sign of life in a mortal body, that is to say, of a state of process and change.' (*The Lamp of Beauty: Writings on Art* by John Ruskin, p 238.)

Le Corbusier, Villa Savoye, Poissy, France, 1928–9.

The building impresses us by its sense of absoluteness and perfection.

Andrei Tarkovsky, *Nostalghia*, 1983. A scene in Domenico's house with leaking roofs, water and eroding materials.

Tarkovsky's eroding cinematic spaces sensitise our senses and emotions through their vulnerability and imperfection.

and Matter' for *Water and Dreams* (1942), he develops the idea of two imaginations:

> By speaking philosophically [...] we can distinguish two sorts of imagination: one that gives life to the formal cause and one that gives life to the material cause – or, more succinctly, a *formal imagination* and a *material imagination* [...] These concepts seem to me indispensable for a complete philosophical study of poetic creation [...] Besides the images of form, so often evoked by psychologists of the imagination, there are [...] images of matter, images that stem *directly from matter*. The eye assigns them names, but only the hand truly knows them.[20] [Italics by Bachelard.]

In another context, the philosopher suggests that images of matter convey deeper emotions than images of form: 'One cannot dream profoundly with *objects*. To dream profoundly, one must dream with *substances*. A poet who begins with a mirror must end with the *water of a fountain* if he wants to present a *complete poetic experience*.'[21] [Italics by Bachelard.]

In its quest for the perfectly articulated and autonomous artefact, the main line of Modernist architecture has preferred materials and surfaces that seek flatness, geometric purity, immaterial abstractness and timeless whiteness (illustration, above left). In Le Corbusier's words, whiteness serves 'the eye of truth',[22] and thus it mediates moral and objective values. The moral implication of whiteness is surprisingly fanatically expressed in his statement: 'Whiteness is extremely moral. Suppose there were a decree requiring all rooms in Paris to be given a coat of whitewash. I maintain that that would be a police task of real stature and a manifestation of high morality, the sign of a great people.'[23]

The surface in Modernist painting, sculpture and architecture is usually treated as an abstracted boundary of the volume, and it has a conceptual and formal rather than sensory essence. The surfaces and the material mass tend to remain mute, as form and volume are given priority; form is vocal, whereas matter remains silent or absent. The preference for geometry and reductive aesthetics further weakens the presence of matter in the same way that a strong figure and contour reading diminishes the interaction of colour between the figure and the ground in the art of painting. All real colourists in painting, such as the Impressionists, or Josef Albers and Mark Rothko, use a weak *gestalt* in order to maximise colour interaction across boundaries.

color intxn for boundaries.
↳blurring & blending

Materials and surfaces surely have a language of their own. Stone speaks of its distant geological origins, its durability and inherent permanence. Brick makes one think of earth and fire, gravity, and the ageless traditions of construction. Bronze evokes the extreme heat of its manufacture, the ancient processes of casting, and the passage of time as measured by its patina. Wood speaks of its two existences and timescales; its first life as a growing tree and the second as a human artefact made by the caring hand of a carpenter or cabinetmaker. These are all materials and surfaces that speak pleasurably of material metamorphoses and layered time. 'One cannot dream profoundly with objects. To dream profoundly, one must dream with substances,' Bachelard argues.[24]

We live in a world of human spirit, ideas and intentions, but we also exist in the world of matter under the quantities and qualities of the physical world. We have two domiciles that constitute an existential singularity: one in the historicity and continuum of human consciousness and emotion, the other in the world of matter and physical phenomena. It is the profound task of the arts and architecture to articulate and express 'how the world touches us' as Merleau-Ponty characterised Paul Cézanne's paintings,[25] and how we touch our world.

Materiality and erosion have been favoured subject matters of contemporary art from Arte Povera and Gordon Matta-Clark to Anselm Kiefer, the films of Andrei Tarkovsky and today's material arts. Materiality, time and destruction are frequently fused; 'Destroying and constructing are equal in importance, and we must have souls for the one and the other [...]', as Paul Valéry states.[26] (illustration, page 47, Andrei Tarkovsky, *Nostalghia*) The installation art of Jannis Kounellis expresses dreams and memories of rusting steel, coal and burlap, whereas Richard Serra's and Eduardo Chillida's authoritative masses of

MATERIAL IMAGINATION: IMAGES OF WATER AND FIRE

We do not dream and imagine only through form, as our imagination is also engaged in substances. Consequently, Bachelard distinguishes between two kinds of imagination: formal imagination and material imagination. He suggests a law of the four elements which classifies various kinds of material imagination by their connections with the elements of antiquity – earth, water, air and fire. In his view the only true opposition is that of water and fire.

Fountain in the Garden of Fin, Kāshān, Iran, 16th century.

Sigurdur Gudmundsson, *Composition*, 1978.

forged and rolled iron awaken bodily experiences of overpowering weight and gravity. These works address directly our skeletal and muscular system: they are communications from the muscles of the sculptor to those of the viewer. The works of bees' wax, pollen and milk by Wolfgang Laib invoke images of spirituality, ritual and ecological concerns, whereas Andy Goldsworthy and Nils-Udo fuse nature and art using materials and elements of nature in their art works.

In Bachelard's view the elements that possess the highest potential to stimulate imagination are fire and water, the only true oppositions (illustrations, above). In fact, Bachelard moved from philosophy of science into the philosophy of the poetic image through his books *The Psychoanalysis of Fire* (1938) and *Water and Dreams* (1942).[27]

> Of all the objects in the world that invoke reverie, a flame calls forth images more readily than any other. It compels us to imagine; when one dreams before a flame, what is perceived is nothing compared to what is imagined. The flame carries its walk of metaphors and images in the most diverse realms of meditation. Take it as the subject of one of the verbs which express life and you will see it enlivens that verb […] of all images, images of the flame – the most artless as well as the most refined, the wisest as well as the most foolish – bear the mark of the poetic. Whoever dreams of a flame is a potential poet.[28]

The images of water are equally varied and poetically evocative. Water is simultaneously the image of life and death, it is also a feminine, maternal element, which can, however, in its most forceful forms, obtain masculine characteristics. More importantly, along with the imagery of fire, water is the most potent image of the imagination. Bachelard speaks of 'a poetics of water' and 'water poets'.[29] 'Perhaps more than any other element', he writes, 'water is a complete poetic reality.'[30] Joseph Brodsky too wrote repeatedly of the specific associative power of water: 'I simply think that water is the image of time', and 'water equals time and provides beauty with its double'.[31]

The presence of water poeticises architecture, as in the architecture of Carlo Scarpa and of Luis Barragán. The encounter of water and stone is entirely metaphysical. In the words of Adrian Stokes, 'The hesitancy of water reveals architectural immobility.'[32] Even entire cities, like Venice, are poeticised by water.

The multi-sensory image

Let us retain and build on the idea that each image has, in effect, a life of its own.[33]

Jacques Aumont, *The Image*, 1997

All artistic structure is essentially 'polyphonic'; it evolves not in a single line of thought, but in several superimposed strands at once. Hence creativity requires a diffuse, scattered kind of attention that contradicts our normal logical habits of thinking.[34]

Anton Ehrenzweig, *The Hidden Order of Art*, 1973

The image is usually thought of in terms of the purely visual and fixed picture, but a characteristic quality of the senses is their tendency to mingle and integrate; a visual image is always accompanied with repercussions connotating experiences in other sense modalities. Besides, there are images in the realms of all the senses. The visual image itself is a constructed fusion of fragmented and discontinuous percepts.

Dynamic vagueness and absence of focus are the conditions of our normal condition of visual perception although we do not usually acknowledge it. Most of us with normal eyesight tend to believe that we see the world around us in focus at all times. The fact is that we see a blur, and only a tiny fraction of the visual field at any time – about one-thousandth of the entire field of vision – is seen distinctly. The field outside this minute, focused centre of vision turns increasingly vague and hazy towards the periphery of the visual field. However, we are unaware of this fundamental lack of accuracy because we constantly scan the field of vision with movements of the eyes – which for the most part remain unconscious and unnoticed – to bring a part of the blurred area at a time into the narrow beam of vision that is brought to a focal pinpoint at the fovea. Experiments have revealed the surprising fact that the unconscious eye movements are not merely aids to clear vision, but an absolute prerequisite of vision altogether. When a subject's gaze is experimentally forced to remain completely fixed on a stationary object, the image of the object disintegrates and keeps disappearing and reappearing again in distorted shapes and fragments. 'Static vision does not exist; there is no seeing without exploring,' the Hungarian-born writer and scholar Arthur Koestler argues.[35] Koestler suggests a cautious analogy between visual scanning and mental scanning, 'between the blurred, peripheral vision outside the focal beam, and the hazy, half-formed notions which accompany thinking on the fringes of consciousness'.[36] He distinguishes focal awareness from peripheral awareness: 'If one attempts to hold fast a mental image or concept – to hold it immobile and isolated, in the focus of awareness, it will disintegrate, like the static, visual image on the fovea ... thinking is never a sharp, neat, linear process.'[37]

Yet, the perception of an image is not an additive entity with auxiliary qualities; it is an integrated experience in which the entity gives meaning to the parts, not vice versa. This dominance of the whole over the detail is again understandable in the evolutionary perspective; it was not meaningful to grasp a detail, say an eye or a tail, but the image of the creature that the detail is part of. Maurice Merleau-Ponty argues strongly for the essential integration of the senses and the instantaneous and holistic character of perception: 'My perception is […] not a sum of visual, tactile and audible givens: I perceive in a total way with my whole being: I grasp a unique structure of the thing, a unique way of being, which speaks to all my senses at once.'[38] Bachelard calls this sensory interaction appropriately 'the polyphony of the senses'.[39]

The synthesising capacity of our perceptual system is truly astonishing. 'The senses translate each other without any need of an interpreter, and are naturally comprehensible without the intervention of any idea,' Merleau-Ponty claims.[40] The multitude of simultaneous percepts is experienced as an integrated entity of the object or setting. Even every architectural setting has

its auditive, haptic, olfactory, and even hidden gustatory qualities, and those properties give the visual percept its sense of fullness and life. Regardless of the immediate character of visual perception, paradoxically we have already unconsciously touched a surface before we become aware of its visual characteristics; we understand its texture, hardness, temperature, moisture instantaneously. In the same way that a painting by Claude Monet, Pierre Bonnard or Henri Matisse evokes a full sense of lived reality, profound buildings are not merely visual images of architectural and aestheticised structures; they are images of life and invitations for particular forms of activities (illustrations, above). True artistic images always possess epic dimensions.

In his book *Art As Experience*,[41] first published in 1934, John Dewey points out the significance of this deep sensory interplay and exchange that we take for granted:

> Qualities of sense, those of touch and taste as well as of sight and hearing, have aesthetic quality. But they have it not in isolation but in their connections: as interacting, not as simple and separate entities. Nor are connections limited to their own kind, colors to colors, sounds with sounds.

The philosopher emphasises the comprehensiveness of the sensory experience:

> The eye, ear and whatever, is only the channel *through* which the total response takes place [...] In seeing a picture, it is not true that visual qualities are as such,

MULTI-SENSORY EXPERIENCE AND SENSUALITY OF LIFE

Great works of art and architecture evoke multi-sensory experiences which put us in an intensely sensuous contact with the imaginary world that they project. Bernard Berenson suggests that works of art evoke 'ideated sensations', and most important of these are tactile experiences. Both Bonnard's painterly image and Aalto's architectural space embrace us and strengthen our connection with their imaginative worlds; the images are tactile as much as they are visual.

Pierre Bonnard, *Nude in the Bath*, 1937. Oil on canvas. Musée du Petit Palais, Paris, France.

Bonnard's paintings project extraordinarily sensuous and tactile spatial experiences; these are paintings to be experienced by the skin.

Alvar Aalto, Villa Mairea, Noormarkku, Finland, 1938–9. Entrance hall and living room.

The space of the living room floor is an architectural continuation of the freely polyrhythmic and multi-sensory space of the forest outside.

or consciously, central, and other qualities arranged about them in an accessory or associated fashion. Nothing could be further from the truth.

The visual image mediates other sensory experiences which may even dominate the nature of the image:

> When we perceive, by means of the eyes as causal aids, the liquidity of water, the coldness of ice, the solidity of rocks, the bareness of trees in winter, it is certain that other qualities than those of the eye are conspicuous and controlling in perception. And it is as certain as anything can be that optical qualities do not stand out by themselves with tactual and emotive qualities clinging to their skirts.

Significantly Dewey points out the innate tendency of sensory experiences to fuse: 'Any sensuous quality tends, because of its organic connections, to spread and fuse.'[42]

The pragmatist philosopher is not referring here to the somewhat exceptional human perceptual capacity of synaesthesia that enables a person to hear colours as sounds or see music as colours, for instance. He speaks of the normal and fundamental quality of our sensory percepts to penetrate into each other and thus render a full existential experience that binds the world and the perceiver into an inseparable unity. We do not just see, hear, touch, smell and taste the world as outside observers, we exist and live in its very intestines. A building is not just a physical structure, as it is also a mental space which structures and articulates our experiences. Meaningful architecture houses us as fully sensing and conscious beings, not as creatures of mere vision. Our house becomes an extension of our body, skin, senses and memory. It is this sense of fullness and completeness that differentiates a life-supporting or 'life-enhancing' – to borrow a notion from Goethe[43] – space from a grim, repulsive or necrophilic space. Yet, the agreeable house presents its ideal of order and interaction undemandingly and courteously. Instead of being alien or commanding, true artistic and architectural works silently and courteously invite us and offer open-ended experiences.

Confirming Dewey's assumptions of the interaction of the sensory realms, today's research in the neurosciences provides swiftly increasing information on the extraordinary interconnectedness and interactions of the various sensory areas of the brain and the entire neural system. The unexpected flexibility of our sensory system has become especially evident in studies of

Worth exploring how they depend on the world.

the sensory capabilities of the blind. 'The world of the blind, of the blinded, it seems, can be especially rich in … in-between states – the intersensory, the metamodal – states for which we have no common language,' argues Oliver Sacks.[44] 'And all of these [...] blend into a single fundamental sense, a deep attentiveness, a slow, almost prehensible attention, a sensuous, intimate being at one with the world which sight, with its quick, flickering, facile quality, continually distracts us from.'[45] The argument of an esteemed medical doctor that vision rather prevents our intimate union with the world than enables a fusion, is most remarkable and thought-provoking for architects, too. Today's forceful effort to seek visually impressive architectural images without a concern for the other sensory realms may well be the very reason why these buildings usually appear so mute, rejecting and lifeless, regardless of their unrestricted play of visual fantasy. They are objects to be looked at and admired, not to be dwelled in or identified with.

how can the senses be hierarchized by the formal qualities of space. Perceptive quality that translate into a state of mind/feeling/tone

In his book World in Fragments, Cornelius Castoriadis emphasises the essential need for coherence in the complexity of the image: 'An image must hold together, it brings together "determinate" elements, presentable elements, and these elements always are found caught up in certain organization and in certain order – otherwise there would be no image, there would simply be chaos.'[46] The poetic image is held together by its creature-like coherence and meaning, which also makes us remember it; or, perhaps, we primarily remember and regenerate its emotional impact instead of its formal properties. In architecture, this quality of cohesion is experienced as the creature-like singularity of the building or space; each profound piece of architecture is a unique representative of a species with a specific and singular anatomy. Paradoxically, this uniqueness suggests a potential universality as in the case of a biological species.

Threshold that activate the diff senses as you walk down w/ this to above ground?

The true miracle of our perception of the world is its very completeness, continuity and constancy, regardless of the fragmentary and discontinuous nature of our perceptions mediated by the different, seemingly incommensurable sensory channels. We do not usually think of the collaboration of touching and seeing, for instance, although seeing itself is a way of touching from a distance without direct physical contact. Besides, the eyes are specialisations of originary skin tissue. The entity of experience is grasped as a coherent and meaningful whole constituted of perceptible and memorable images. Normally we manage to live in a unified and continuous world, whereas in certain sensory and mental failures, such as schizophrenia, this healthy integration is lost.

Diff tempo of the day? In a subway stn.

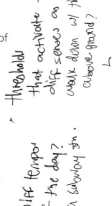

The image as a condensation

I do not doubt but the majesty and beauty of the world are latent in any iota of the world …

I do not doubt there is far more in trivialities, insects, vulgar persons, slaves, dwarfs, weeds, rejected refuse, than I have supposed …

I do not doubt interiors have their interiors … eyesight has another eyesight, and the hearing another hearing, and the voice another voice.[47]

Walt Whitman, 'Faith Poem' from *Leaves of Grass*, 1856

The notion of 'abstraction' is commonly used to explain the power of the artistic image and, in particular, the nature of 'non-figurative', 'non-representational' or geometric imagery in art. In my view, the notions of abstraction and 'non-representational' are unfortunate and misleading, as they suggest that such images are without content, context, reference and meaning, and that they are detached from the life-world. What is usually labelled as 'abstraction' in an artistic representation is, in fact, an extreme condensation of imagery, experience, signification and meaning. Instead of abstracting, in the sense of taking away or reducing, the artistic image calls for a compression of a multitude of percepts, memories, associations and existential meanings into an experiential singularity.

On the other hand, the profound 'non-representational' image surely represents, i.e. it invokes and stands for aspects of the life-world, but not through an explicit convention or code, such as perspectival or figurative representation. Anton Ehrenzweig, one of the most perceptive psychoanalytic interpreters of the unconscious contents and processes in art, points to the essential depth dimension in artistic creation:

> In our abstract art there is a dramatic short-circuit between its high
> sophistication and love of geometry on the one hand and an almost oceanic
> lack of differentiation obtaining in its matrix in the unconscious mind. The 'full'
> emptiness of great abstract art may be dependent on its close link with a cluster
> of incompatible images (serial structures) pressing around in it on the level of
> unconscious vision.

In Ehrenzweig's view, an artistic abstraction becomes empty when it loses its association with the unconscious:

> These conflicting images cancelled each other out on their way up to consciousness and so produced the misleading superficial impression of emptiness and abstraction. Abstraction becomes truly empty whenever it is dissociated from its unconscious matrix.[48]

Instead of moving away from life, artistic abstractions penetrate into the very essence and heart of phenomena and experience. Instead of being devoid of meaning, their signification is intensified and generalised through the creative process of experiential condensation. This metamorphosis takes place in an intense interplay between the unconscious and conscious mental faculties, and between generality and specificity. This is a process of compression and distillation, not of distancing or diluting. Ehrenzweig makes the significant argument: 'Scientific abstraction differs from an empty generalization in the way in which potent abstract art differs from empty ornament.'[49] (illustrations, below) If the unconscious mental reverberations, undercurrents and connections with a sense of life are missing, the work remains a mere play with intellectualised elements of visual design, a mere visual decoration; the

image is born without meaning and a sense of life. Meaning in art implies a connection with the life-world and a sense of completeness and fullness, not a theoretical proposition, verbal argument, explanation or invented narrative. We do not initially project the story on the image, it is the image that reveals its narrative to us. The image does not need to be explained, either it opens its secrets to us, or it does not.

Brancusi points out that a true artistic abstraction is the result of a long and laboursome process, not an a priori attitude, or a preconceived image: 'Simplicity is not an end of art, but one arrives at simplicity in spite of oneself, in approaching the real essence of things, simplicity is at bottom complexity and one must be nourished on its essence to understand its significance.'[50]

Due to its inherently constructed, rationalised and geometric essence, architecture often remains as a coordinated and aestheticised technical assembly, incapable of evoking images and associations of poeticised life. High-Tech architecture, for instance, tends to degenerate into pure technological rationality, and the stylistically deliberate architectural Minimalism easily turns into retinal reduction and a superficial suggestiveness of a forceful but fabricated and arbitrary image. All meaningful architectural images speak of the continuum of human culture and life, not merely of technology, reason or distinct aesthetic preferences.

It seems paradoxical, indeed, that architecture, the art form which arises directly from activities of life and deliberately serves the practical purposes of life, would have turned into the art form that is often most devoid of life. The Dutch filmmaker Jan Vrijman asks appropriately: 'Why is it that architecture and architects, unlike film and filmmakers, are so little interested in people during the design process? Why are they so theoretical, so distant from life in general?'[51]

A profound artistic image projects a sense of rootedness, completeness, life and magic. It speaks with the authority of an entire life-experience. It short-circuits our faculties of rational understanding and feeling, as well as the categories of life and knowledge, reality and dream, beauty and meaning. This logical short-circuit gives rise to the 'aura' of the work of art that Walter Benjamin recognised.[52] Poetic images arise from a sense of life and they are generators of live experiences.

IMAGES OF CONDENSED MEANING

'Scientific abstraction differs from an empty generalization in the way in which potent abstract art differs from empty ornament,' Anton Ehrenzweig argues. Both science and art seek expressions that condense a multitude of meanings into a singular image or formulation. Even in the sciences, aesthetic criteria have a significant role.

Albert Einstein at the blackboard.

'In a lifetime Einstein connected light to time, time to space, energy to matter, matter to space, and space to gravitation.' (J Bronowski, The Ascent of Man, 1973.)

Kazimir Malevich, Black Square, oil on canvas, 1913. State Russian Museum, St Petersburg, Russia.

The Malevich painting is an iconic abstraction and condensation of meaning.

The archetypal image in architecture

Every great vision of the world must start with the cosmic egg.[53]

Gaston Bachelard, *The Flame of a Candle*, 1988

They [archetypes] are pieces of life itself – images that are integrally connected to the living individual by the bridge of the emotions.[54]

Carl G Jung, *Man and His Symbols*, 1968

Images and associations met with in dreams, correlatives of which can be found in primitive thought, myths and rites, were called 'archaic remnants of the mind' by Sigmund Freud. CG Jung later gave these archaic images the name 'archetype'.[55] These historical associations operate as a link between the world of the consciousness and the unconscious world of instinct. Jung defines archetypes as both patterns and emotions that tend to generate certain kinds of associations and meanings. In essence, archetypes do not have fixed, closed symbolic connotations, because they act as generators of associations and emotions, and they encourage constant reinterpretation. They belong to life itself and are inextricably linked with the individual through his/her emotions, as Jung remarked.

Archetypes are also the essential ingredients of the usually formally simple language of architecture. Sinclair Gauldie expressly assumes the existence of an archetypal architectural language which also gives architecture its artistic permanence: 'The building which, long after the fashionable idioms of its time have degenerated into clichés, still continues to contribute some memorable quality to human life, is the building which draws its communicative force from the unchanging emotional associations in the architectural language, those which are most deeply rooted in the common sensory experience of humanity.'[56] In the words of Bachelard, 'the house is one of the greatest powers of integration for the thoughts, memories and dreams of mankind'.[57]

Adrian Stokes' statement, 'Architectural forms are a language confined to the joining of a few ideographs of immense ramification,' also points towards the archetypal essence of the language of architecture.[58] Independently of the idea of archetype, it is evident that architecture articulates primary human experiences of being-in-the-world, such as gravity and mass, horizontality and verticality, earth and sky, centre and periphery, nature and culture, landscape

THE BASIC GEOMETRIC IMAGES IN ART

Artistic images are usually structured by means of basic geometric gestalt. The basic geometric shapes have their symbolic connotations, but more important than their conventional meanings are their conceptual and visual organising powers. Architectural history from the Egyptian pyramids to today's Minimalist architecture reveals the significant and constant role of geometric images.

The three images show the persistence of the square, triangle and circle in art and architecture irrespective of cultural and historical context.

The Universe, painting by the 18th-century Japanese Zen artist Sengai.

Le Corbusier, 'Trois rappels à Messieurs les Architectes' ('Three Reminders to Messrs Architects'), *Vers une architecture*, 1923.

The cover of the *Bauhaus* journal, 1928, illustrated by Herbert Bayer. (From Kraus reprint, 1976.)

Trois rappels à MM. les architectes.

and artifice, individuality and collectivity, past and present. The most fundamental encounter mediated by architecture is the confrontation of the self and the world. All other art forms activate momentarily these fundamental existential dialectics, but architecture structures them as our permanent condition of life.

In the visual arts in general, and particularly in architecture, the basic forms dominate – the circle, the square, the triangle, as well as the basic orientations and numbers – either explicitly or as hidden images of order and organisation beneath the surface of conscious observation (illustrations, above and left). The basic geometric shapes have a host of symbolic meanings through history in various cultures, but their purely perceptual qualities and impact seem to be more important, particularly for their use in modern times. The circle, for instance, both focuses perception and energy in a centripetal manner, but it also expands and emanates energy centrifugally. At the same time, the circle is a symbol of the self, expressing all the dimensions of the psyche, including the man-nature relationship. In primitive sun worship and in modern religion, in myths and dreams, in the mandalas of Tibetan monks, in town plans, and in the circular systems of early astronomers, it always indicates the unity of life.[59] The square, in turn, is an expression of earthbound static materialism, the body and reality. The alchemic attempt to fuse the images of square and circle was, symbolically, a desire to unite the self and the world, the realm of man and the universe.

Of the cardinal numbers, four is crucial in biblical exegesis.[60] The number four also appears in the following contexts: the four rivers of Paradise, the four Fathers of the Latin Church, four-level exegetics, the four cardinal virtues, the four cardinal directions, the four quadrants of the world. In the language of architecture the number four also has a central position, such as the four quadrants of the square subdivided by two axes. Numbers and their relationships also have a significant role in the long history of Pythagorean harmonics from Vitruvius Pollio to Aulis Blomstedt.

A figure, image or object can also have a special meaning as a basic unit of an artistic or architectural composition and construction, such as the square or the cube. Sol LeWitt, the American artist, gives an interesting explanation of his use of the cube as the basic unit in much of his work; he uses the cube because of its relative neutrality and inexpressiveness.

> The most interesting characteristic of the cube is that it is relatively uninteresting. Compared to any other three-dimensional form, the cube lacks any aggressive force, implies no motion, and is least emotive. Therefore it is the best form to use as a basic unit for any more elaborate function, the grammatical device from which the work may proceed.

In his view, the cube has no connotations beyond being a geometric figure:

> Because it is standard and universally recognized, no intention is required of the viewer. It is immediately understood that the cube represents the cube, a geometric figure that is uncontestably itself. The use of the cube obviates the necessity of inventing another form and reserves its use for invention.[61]

In my view, an artistic or architectural work does not draw its emotional power from deliberate and explicit symbolisation. Symbolism only fixes the image to a distinct context, such as mythical, religious or ideological connotations, but this connection does not provide the work with emotive power beyond acknowledging the convention, or a reference to a system or tradition of belief. Andrei Tarkovsky's films are usually interpreted as symbolically charged cinematic images. Yet, the director explicitly rejects the idea of deliberate symbolisation:

> Whenever I declare that there are no symbols or metaphors in my films, those present express incredulity. They persist in asking again and again, for instance, what rain signifies in my films; why does it figure in film after film; and why the repeated images of wind, fire, water? … Of course, rain can just be seen as bad weather, whereas I use it to create a particular aesthetic setting in which to steep the action of the film. But that is not at all the same thing as bringing nature into my films as symbols of something else.[62]

Most architects would surely agree with the film director on the secondary role of symbolism in their work regardless of whether symbolising elements can be detected in it. A symbolic connotation may, however, simultaneously connect the work with a source of archetypal associative power and give it a sense of unexplainable fullness. Yet, the true force and meaning of an artistic work always arises from its rich unconscious soil and motifs, not surface symbols or conventions.

Architecture as mandala

The mandala, an object of concentrated meditation, which represents the cosmos in relation to divine forces, is a special configuration of the basic forms of circle, square and triangle (which appears particularly in Indian yantras). The mandala is usually associated with Oriental cultures, but abstract mandalas also appear in Christian art, such as the rose windows of cathedrals. Even the haloes of Christ and the Christian saints in religious paintings and the image of Christ surrounded by the four Evangelists can be regarded as mandalas.[63] In the history of architecture and town planning, the mandala is also of great significance; buildings and cities can often be seen as geometric and spatial mandalas.

An interesting example of the squaring of the circle, the symbolic joining of the man-built world with the universe, is Plutarch's account of the geometrically contradictory founding rites of Rome, the *Urbs Quadrata*.[64] These rites were based on the ritual application of circles. The founding rites and early maps of many towns around the world are based on the overlapping of idealised images of the circle and square, regardless of the actual local geographical facts, such as the idealised and largely fictitious ancient maps of Jerusalem. The same archetypal significance of the basic forms was usually inherent in the orientation and siting of cult buildings. These rites established the ritual integration of the cosmos and man and the demarcation of the psychic centre axis mundi, or man's basic orientation in space and time.

Certain figures or shapes, such as the *vesica piscis*, the ovoid figure that was commonly used as the background of Christ in medieval paintings and sculptures, also derive from the early use of circular geometries in ancient temple founding rituals.

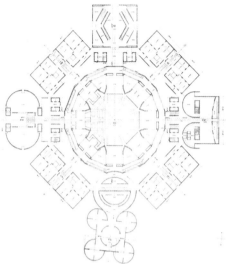

The Dogon tribe of Mali has condensed its creation myth and world picture, as well as its rules of conduct and daily life derived from them, into the image of a symbolic granary, or a celestial ark.[65] This image forms a three-dimensional mandala consisting of a combination of circles and squares (see illustration, page 122, Drawing of the Dogon Mythical Ark). The image functions as a key to the Dogon interpretation of the world and its origins. The four stairways of this cosmic representation, for instance, were used as a system of classification for animal species and plants.

The mandala essence of architectural structures is evident in the geometries of Indian temples as well as countless Western buildings of the Classical era. Even numerous contemporary buildings, such as Louis I Kahn's Parliament Building in Dhaka, Bangladesh, evoke the mandala image. The aspiration to fuse the cosmic and the human, divine and mortal, spiritual and material, combined with the use of systems of proportion and measure deriving simultaneously from the cosmic order and human figure, gave architectural geometries their meaning and deep sense of spiritual life.

The ostensible abstractness of modern architecture also acquires its expressive power and emotional effect from the unconscious meanings of the forms it uses. However, in mannerist modernity, forms have often lost their archetypal, cosmic and symbolic meanings, and they remain as elements of mere visual

The mandala is first and
foremost an Eastern
meditation figure, but
architectural compositions
can often be interpreted as
mandalas: intense geometric
images that structure the
experience of space and
place. In fact, architectural
structures are essentially
three-dimensional and spatial
mandalas. The mandala
character is frequently
obvious in, for example, Frank
Lloyd Wright's and Mies
van der Rohe's buildings.
Although the basic mandala
image is a centralised and
focusing gestalt, many
modern architectural images,
such as Mies van der Rohe's
Country House (c 1934), can
be regarded as asymmetrical
and dynamic spatial
mandalas, modern devices for
spatial meditation.

Mandala of Yamantaka,
Tibetan Tanka.

The Mandala is a sacred
diagram that represents the
structure of the universe.
The Sanskrit word 'mandala'
means circle and centre.

Louis I Kahn, National
Assembly Building, Dhaka,
Bangladesh, 1962–74. Floor
plan.

The prayer hall (a perfect 20
metre cube) deviates slightly
from the coordinates of the
Assembly Building proper as it
is oriented in accordance with
the Islamic canon.

aesthetics without an echo in our unconscious and collective memory. In contemporary architecture, measures and proportions usually serve only instrumental purposes, and they arise from the architect's individual sense of harmony, but they have entirely lost their metaphysical and cosmic connections.

The reality and unreality of the artistic image

All artistic images simultaneously take place in two realities and their suggestive power derives from this very tension between the real and the suggested, the perceived and the imagined. In the act of experiencing a work, the artistic image shifts from the physical and material existence into a mental and imaginary reality. The inability to grasp the essence of an artistic work usually arises from the viewer's incapability to project and experience the imaginary reality of the work. However, the two existences do not cancel out or exclude each other as they maintain a dynamic and dialectic relationship.

In her delightful book *Dreaming by the Book,* Elaine Scarry argues that the literary arts differ from all the other art forms in not possessing direct sensory imageries, only printed letters on a page.[66] Consequently, the reader is obliged to create the imagery in his/her imagination in accordance with the writer's instructions contained in the text. This is certainly true, but also in the other art forms, such as painting, architecture and dance, the factual sensory imagery of the work gives rise to an imaginative level that constitutes the poetic and affective reality of the work.

Sartre makes an intriguing argument on the two existences of the artistic image and their metamorphoses in the art form of acting: 'It is not the Prince of Denmark who becomes real in the actor, but the actor who becomes *unreal* as the Prince.'[67] In his essay on the painter Balthus, Guy Davenport, the poet, makes an interesting parallel comment on the relative reality or unreality of painted figures, as if even they posed in their roles as actors: 'He [Balthus] has the immediacy of a naive painter. Picasso's people are all actors, wearers of masks, mediators, like Picasso himself, between reality and illusion. Pierrot, woman as artist's model, the Ballet Russe, the Commedia dell'Arte dominate his entire oeuvre.'[68]

Also architecture occupies two domains simultaneously: the reality of its tectonic and material construction, and the abstracted, idealised and spiritual dimension of its artistic imagery. There is yet another simultaneous duality in architecture: its essence as a structure of utility and as a proposition of an aesthetic ideal. Every meaningful building resists gravity, the elements and wear, but it also presents an idealised order and a lived existential metaphor. The great houses of Modernism, such as Le Corbusier's Villa Savoye (1928–9), express a view of the world, concept of space, the dialogue between nature and artifice and a distinct way of life through an architectural language of abstraction (illustration, page 47, Le Corbusier, Villa Savoye, Poissy, France). Buildings are simultaneously here in the world of physical facts and causalities, and elsewhere in the world of ideas, geometries and artistic expressions. They have a double task: the practical function of life and activities, and the psychic function of establishing our mental foothold in the lived reality. I shall return to the dual life of the image in Chapter 4, 'The Dual Existence of the Poetic Image'.

The unconscious image

Artistic images seem to address directly our existential sense, and have their impact through our bodily being, before they are cerebrally registered or understood. An artistic work may have a forceful mental and emotional impact, yet remain forever without an intellectual explanation. '[T]he image has touched the depths before it stirs the surface', as Bachelard remarks.[69] Giorgione's *Tempesta* (c 1506) presents its innocently seducing scene and poeticises the onlooker's imagination, although the meaning of the allegorical staging will remain forever an enigma.

Wondering how certain buildings have a sudden, deep impact on his mind, Colin St John Wilson, the architect of the British Library, explains the mental power of architectural imagery on our minds:

> It is as if I am being manipulated by some subliminal code, not to be translated into words, which acts directly on the nervous system and imagination, at the same time stirring intimations of meaning with vivid spatial experience as though they were one thing. It is my belief that the code acts so directly and vividly upon us because it is strangely familiar; it is in fact the first language we ever learned, long before words, and which is now recalled to us through art, which alone holds the key to revive it …[70]

Architecture articulates the characteristics and qualities of our fundamental existential experiences and feelings. It even addresses and touches upon some of our most basic prenatal experiences of enclosure, security, intimacy and pleasure. It mediates between the self and the world, self and the other, and it re-structures the earliest memories of our basic dialectics of connectedness and separation.

The creative impulse often progresses semi-automatically, as if the images and words would appear independently of the maker's will and intention. The artist/maker often feels that the image world that he/she is creating has pre-existed and the creative process is a matter of revealing what has always existed, rather than giving existence and form to a reality created by him/her. Jackson Pollock confessed that he painted his canvases in a kind of trance:

> When I am in my painting I am not aware of what I am doing. It is only after a sort of 'get acquainted' period that I see what I have been about. I have no fears about making changes, destroying the image etc., because the painting has a life of its own. I try to let it come through. It is only when I lose contact with the painting that the result is a mess. Otherwise there is pure harmony, an easy give and take, and the painting comes out well.[71]

Psychoanalytic theories of creativity and the creative process explain these intriguing phenomena as an interplay between our conscious and unconscious faculties. During the arduous process of making, unconscious experiences, memories and motives directly influence the emerging work and secretly become part of its essential contents. The artistic work is a struggle – or collaboration – between the conscious ego and the suppressed unconscious contents of the mind. As a consequence a successful work always contains more than the artist/architect consciously put into it, and the work appears to have emerged semi-autonomously.

In his seminal study of the creative and artistic impact, *The Hidden Order of Art* (1967), Anton Ehrenzweig distinguishes two kinds of attention: the conscious attention which follows conscious intentions, thoughts and the perceptual principles revealed by gestalt psychology, on the one hand, and a 'multi-dimensional', 'polyphonic' and scattered unconscious attention, which is capable of grasping complex and conflicting entities, on the other.[72] He also suggests the existence of unconscious processes of visual and auditory scanning[73] that succeed to grasp complex, field-like images through the unfocused perception of the eyes and ears. In Ehrenzweig's view, these processes of unconscious artistic vision and hearing momentarily take over in the creative process.

Architectural tasks are almost always so complex, consisting of logically irreconcilable and conflicting ingredients – points of departure and intentions, practicalities and mental ideas – that it cannot at all be resolved rationally; an architectural task can be confronted only through an embodied and existential, simultaneously rational and poetic encounter which bypasses logistical barriers and categories. Alvar Aalto reasons: 'In every case, opposites must be reconciled [...] Almost every formal assignment involves dozens, often hundreds, sometimes thousands of conflicting elements that can be forced into functional harmony only by an act of will. This harmony cannot be achieved by any other means than art.'[74]

The metaphor

Metaphor is primarily a form of cognition rather than a trope or figure of speech. Further, metaphor as a cognitive tool can operate unconsciously, so that a metaphoric process is one aspect of the unconscious mind.[75]

Arnold H Modell, *Imagination and the Meaningful Brain*, 2006

Metaphors evoke one another and are coordinated more than sensations, so that a poetic mind is purely and simply a syntax of metaphors.[76]

Gaston Bachelard, *On Poetic Imagination and Reverie*, 1998

Metaphor relies on what has been experienced before and therefore transforms the strange into the familiar. Without metaphor we cannot imagine what it is to be someone else, we cannot imagine the life of the Other.[77]

Cynthia Ozick, quoted in AH Modell, *Imagination and the Meaningful Brain*, 2006

Aristotle emphasised the centrality of the metaphor in thinking. 'The greatest excellence [in the use of words] is to be happy in the use of metaphor; for it is this alone which cannot be acquired, and which, consisting in a quick discernment of resemblances, is a certain mark of genius,' he argues in *Poetics*.[78]

Many of today's scholars in various art forms continue to stress the significance of the metaphor as a crucial tool of thinking and communication. 'The development of consciousness in human beings is inseparably connected with the use of metaphor. Metaphors are not merely peripheral decorations or even useful models, they are fundamental forms of our condition,' argues Iris Murdoch, novelist and philosopher.[79] Yehuda Amichai goes even further in the value that he assigns to the metaphor as a constitutive factor in humanity: 'Metaphor is the great human revolution, at least on a par with the invention of the wheel … Metaphor is a weapon in the hand-to-hand struggle with reality.'[80]

Metaphor is traditionally associated with its verbal and literary use. Yet, metaphors arise directly from our bodily being in the physical world and our body-centred mode of perception and cognition as George Lakoff and Mark Johnson reveal in *Metaphors We Live By*.[81] Arnold H Modell points out the fundamental multi-sensory and embodied nature of the metaphor: 'Metaphor formation is intrinsically multimodal, as it must engage visual, auditory, and kinaesthetic inputs. In addition, metaphor formation must access unconscious memory.'[82] Introducing the notion of 'corporeal imagination', Modell further emphasises its embodied essence: 'As a mode of cognition, metaphor is doubly embodied; first as an unconscious neural process, and, accordingly, in that metaphors are generated from bodily feelings, so that it is possible to speak of a corporeal imagination.'[83]

There is a temptation to connect the two notions of image and metaphor, but Bachelard makes a fundamental distinction between them.

> Academic psychology hardly deals with the subject of the poetic image, which is often mistaken for simple metaphor. Generally, in fact, the word *image*, in the works of psychologists, is surrounded by confusion: we see images, we reproduce images, we retain images in our memory. [In the psychologising view] the image is everything except a direct product of the imagination … I propose, on the contrary, to consider the imagination as a major power of human nature.[84] [Italics by Bachelard.]

Artistic images of various aspects of the world are metaphoric representations which momentarily become part of our mental landscape. In fact, in the encounter of a work of art, a double projection and binding takes place: we project aspects of ourselves on the work, and the work becomes part of us. The metaphor evokes, guides, strengthens and maintains our thoughts, emotions and associations.

Architectural structures are simultaneously utilitarian constructions for specific purposes, and spatial and material images of our being-in-the-world. They are lived metaphors, that mediate between the world and the human realm of life, immensity and intimacy, past and present. In order to give structure and meaning to our existential experience, the art of architecture projects externalised mental structures and images which we occupy and live in. Architectural metaphors are usually neither consciously conceived nor intellectually identified, as they guide and condition our actions and emotions through unconscious and embodied channels. Architectural metaphors are grounded in the very faculties of our being-in-the-world, and they are grasped by our existential and embodied sense rather than the intellect.

I wish to state clearly that I do not support architectural nostalgia or conservatism. I speak for an architecture that arises from the acknowledgement of its historical, cultural, societal and mental soil. When visiting Louis Kahn's Assembly Building in Dhaka, Bangladesh, I was deeply impressed by the extraordinary architectural power of the Parliament Complex in creating a sense of place and centre that exudes cultural and metaphysical meanings and elevates the human spirit. It has the focusing power of a mandala, a meditation image. This architecture is uncompromisingly of our time, yet it echoes and revitalises deep layers of history and culture, and succeeds in evoking societal pride and hope through its powerful metaphoric essence. This architecture evokes historical images all the way from the Karnak Temple of ancient Egypt and the *gravitas* of Roman architecture, but it is simultaneously a healing promise of reconciliation and justice for the future (illustrations, opposite).

Nurur Rahman Khan, a Bangladeshi architect, movingly connects Kahn's architecture with the local culture:

> Our assembly building today has become so ingrained as part of our national consciousness over the last few decades that it seems to have had no beginning, no real starting point. Rather, it appears to have always been there ... that what was always in our mind, what was always a part of us. Our assembly building is so close to our hearts and memories that it seems to have acquired that quality of timelessness and eternity which comes hand in hand with the identity and our perception thereof of being a Bangladeshi.[85]

Khaleed Ashraf, another local architect, describes Kahn's architectural epiphany as follows:

> In the Assembly Building [...] major architectural streams, Roman Renaissance, Mughal, and Modern, seem to have converged – not in a synthesis but as a

THE INTEGRATING IMAGERY OF ARCHITECTURE

Modern and contemporary architectures have been repeatedly accused of being devoid of emotional and mental impact. Yet, numerous architectural masterpieces of the modern era move us as much as any of the great works of history. The power of architecture lies in its deeply unconscious and collectively identifiable mental content that addresses us through embodied imagery and metaphor.

The profound works always evoke a consciousness of the past, as if they were incarnations of history. This experience of temporal depth arises from a 'historical sense' – to use a notion of TS Eliot – rather than any specific historical period or precedent.

Louis I Kahn, Hypostyle Hall, Temple of Ammon, Karnak, Egypt, 1951. Charcoal on paper, 29.2 × 37.5 cm. Collection of Sue Ann Kahn.

The Karnak temple exudes a unique architectural force because it is as much solid matter as it is space.

Louis I Kahn, Sher-E-Bangla Nagar National Assembly Hall, Dhaka, Bangladesh, 1962–74.

The geometry of Louis Kahn's architecture projects a primordial power and sense of authority.

palimpsest – in one single architectural event […] Long before its functional occupation as a political 'citadel', it became inscribed in the collective mind, paradoxically through its 'ruinous' image, as an emblem of things to come. Like an epic, which is no longer of our time, but of a cosmic time, and […] it spoke of essential things, things around which life coheres and seeks meaning.[86]

It is truly remarkable that citizens of a developing Islamic nation can sincerely praise a piece of uncompromised contemporary architecture, created by a Western architect of Jewish background. This gives confidence in the continued reconciliatory and empowering potential of true architecture as well as in the inexhaustible mental power of great architectural metaphors.

Image, affect and empathy

Empathy is an unconscious process in which the individual uses his own body as a template that enables him to 'feel' into the other's experience.[87]

Vittorio Gallese, quoted in AH Modell, *Imagination and the Meaningful Brain*, 2006

Mimetic skill or mimesis rests on the ability to produce conscious, self-initiated, representational acts that are intentional but not linguistic.[88]

Merlin Donald, quoted in AH Modell, *Imagination and the Meaningful Brain*, 2006

In Jean-Paul Sartre's view, an image in itself possesses no emotive power; the image itself cannot be enticing, comforting or nauseating, for instance. Richard

Kearney explains the Sartrean understanding of the image: 'It is not the image that is persuasive, erotic or disgusting. It is we who persuade, excite and disgust *ourselves* by the very act in which we construct the image […] An image is an unreality which has no qualities unless given by us' (italics by Kearney).[89] The emotive content arises in the encounter with the work and the viewer's projection of aspects of him/herself on the work. We persuade, excite and disgust ourselves through the act of confronting and constructing the image and associating with it. In the Sartrean existentialist view, an image is an unreality and it has no qualities without a human experience that projects distinct properties and qualities on the image. Asserting the idea that an artistic image has to be brought to life, Kearney concludes, 'a picture is dead until it is imagined'.[90]

When reading Dostoevsky's *Crime and Punishment*, the reader gradually constructs the entire city of St Petersburg with its countless streets, alleys, buildings, rooms, shadowed corners, inhabitants and their varied fates. The scene of Mikolka beating his tortured horse to death is emotionally unbearable, as the reader sees and experiences this brutal scene so vividly that his/her entire ethical sense revolts against this obscene cruelty. The reader even develops a feeling of guilt for not being able to prevent this atrocity. All significant artistic images evoke ethical attitudes.

The view, that in our role as readers/listeners/viewers/dwellers we project the emotional content and mental meaning onto the artistic image, helps us to understand how even primordial works of art can have their full sense of life and actuality through the void of thousands of years. 'An artist is worth a thousand centuries,' as Paul Valéry argues perceptively.[91]

Experiencing emotional content in an image implies an identification with the object and a projection of self on the image. It is known that the newborn human infant shows an innate capacity to imitate motor actions. Even one hour after birth, infants already imitate tongue protrusion and other facial and manual gestures. Vittorio Gallese and Giacomo Rizzolatti's discovery of mirror neurons proposes that 'self-initiated actions and the individual's perception of the identical actions performed by another evoke the same neural response. An important aspect of the observation is that it is not the visual perception of the object that is activated in mirror neurons as these neurons fire only when a specific action is observed'.[92] These observations give rise to the assumption that the brain is intrinsically relational. 'This research suggests that we use our bodies as a template that enables us to feel our way into the other's experience. This supports the contention that the roots of empathy are in the body, and as with projective identification, this process occurs unconsciously.'[93]

The fact that we have the capacity to grasp spatially the depicted reality of two-dimensional images as well as depicted action and movement, combined with the psychoanalytically verified phenomenon of projective identification and the current discovery of mirror neurons, suggests a basis for our mysterious capacity to experience an intense emotive and affective relationship with artistic images. The experience of having been moved to tears by a painting, piece of music or architectural space, is evidently valorised by the recent discoveries in the field of neurology. Gallese assumes that there may even be other similar mechanisms in the brain besides mirror neurons that explain the neural ground of intersubjectivity.[94]

The collaged image

Age-old walls with their scratches, traces and stains, as well as billboards of torn and layered remains of posters and advertisements, are often intriguingly suggestive unintentional collages. Collage and assemblage are the most characteristic modern and contemporary artistic techniques along with the cinematic montage. Collage creates a dense non-linear and associative

EMPATHY IN ART AND ARCHITECTURE

We experience works of art and architecture as horrifying, melancholic, consoling, invigorating and welcoming, due to an unconscious projection and exchange of emotions and affect. The artistic image conditions our whole mental and bodily being to project uncontrolled feelings on the work and receive them back as if they were qualities of the material work itself.

Titian, *Apollo and Marsyas*, c 1575, 212 × 207 cm. National Museum, Kromeriz, Czech Republic.

The painted scene of Marsyas the satyr being skinned alive in Apollo's revenge is almost unbearable to look at because one feels one's own skin being peeled off. The emotive power of the image reveals how deeply we internalise and identify with poetic images.

Alvar Aalto, Tuberculosis Sanatorium, Paimio, 1929–33.

The arrival image of Alvar Aalto's Paimio Sanatorium welcomes the patient and exudes a therapeutic air of healing and optimism.

narrative field through initially unrelated aggregates, as the fragments obtain new roles and significations through the context and dialogue with other image fragments. The ingredients suggest varying origins and histories and the implied discontinuities provide suggestive shifts and gaps in the narrative or the logic of the image. A special category of the collage are images that hover between visual and verbal, painterly and poetic, material and conceptual expressions, such as the lyrical textual collages of the Czech poet-painter Jiři Kolař (1914–2002) (illustration, above left).

The notion of the collage also applies to architecture. Layers of different uses and alterations through time in a building or setting suggest a condensed and dense time, and the deliberate technique of collage. The renovation of a building inevitably gives rise to the juxtaposition of contrasting structures, forms, technologies, materials and details in a collage manner. The deliberate juxtaposition of old and new speaks of several lives and cultural eras of the structure. The original architectural expression and symbolism may well

Rainer Maria Rilke uses
the beautiful notion
Dinggedicht for poetry
that is based on objects.
Collage and assemblage are
characteristically modern
artistic methods that create
associative connections
between found objects and
fragmented images.

Renovation and reuse of
buildings often introduces a
poetic counterpoint between
different functions, materials
and architectural languages.
Renovation projects in
architecture frequently
convey a theatrical ambience;
the new serves as a ground
and framing for the old, and
vice versa.

Jiří Kolář, *Il congresso degli
uccelli*, 80 × 60 cm, 1963.

The poetic imagery of the
Czech poet/artist's collages
is suspended between words
and pictures, sentences and
objects.

Carlo Scarpa, Castelvecchio
Museum, Verona, 1956–64.
(In collaboration with C
Maschietto and A Rudi).

Scarpa was the ultimate
master of renovation projects
that layer architectural
messages from different
periods and styles.

be in dramatic conflict with the adapted use. Carlo Scarpa's renovation of
Castelvecchio in Verona (1956–64) (illustration, opposite page, right), Sverre
Fehn's transformation of the ruins of the Bishop's Mansion at Hamar into
the Hedmark Cathedral Museum (1967–79) and David Chipperfield's recent
reconstruction of the destroyed Neues Museum in Berlin (2009) are among
the most impressive examples of architectural collages to have emerged
through thoughtful and sensitive renovation. Such tasks call for constant value
judgement and concern for authenticity, and a sensitivity to understand and
create architectural dialogues through styles and time. Due to their inherent
layering and multi-thematic character, renovation projects often acquire a
distinctly theatrical ambience.

The artistic strategy of collage inevitably suggests layers of time, and found
architectural fragments or ruins invoke the nostalgic presence of time; ruins
are an architectural *memento mori*. The strategy of collage has also been used
in the design of entirely new buildings for the purpose of creating a sense of
history and duration. Sir John Soane's House (now a museum) at Lincoln's
Inn Fields in London (1792–1824) is a dense collage of architectural motifs
and historical fragments (illustration, page 74, left). The architect was so
obsessed with the idea of an architectural ruin, that after having finished the
construction, he wrote a report of his house as experienced in a ruined state
through the eyes of a future antiquarian.[95]

Among the architects of the modern era, Alvar Aalto was often interested in
creating the experience of temporal duration and the ambience of historical
settings by means of subliminal suggestions of remains of previous cultures
or ruins, such as the brick collage of his Experimental House at Muuratsalo
(1952–3) (illustration, page 74, right). This tectonic collage around a courtyard
suggests that the brick walls are built of the remains of a previous structure
on the site; in fact they are made of discarded bricks from his construction
site of the Säynätsalo Town Hall (1948–52) in the vicinity and of numerous tile
variations from his other earlier and contemporaneous projects. This imagery
creates an experience of tactile time and a feeling of rootedness, nostalgia
and longing. The Villa Mairea in Noormarkku (1938–9) is another example
of the architect's collage technique, in this case an assemblage of image
motifs that refer to Finnish vernacular traditions, international modernity and
Japanese traditional architecture (illustrations, pages 52, right, and 85, right).
The design deliberately collages numerous materials, formal themes and detail
elaborations and is quite evidently related to the Cubist idea of collage.

Images of incompleteness and destruction

Incomplete and eroding surfaces and forms initiate and stimulate dreaming
in the same way that an ink-blot figure in the personality test devised by
the Swiss psychiatrist Hermann Rorschach (1884–1922) invites figural
interpretations. These images and their interpretations open up channels
to hidden mental worlds. This tendency to see familiar or alien things in a
fundamentally shapeless or 'thingless' image is frequently deployed in the arts.
Our sensory and perceptual system is oriented towards constant scanning of
the perceptual field for potential meaning; this inherent function of the sensory
and neural organisation can be understood in a bio-historical perspective. The
capacity and immediacy of grasping meaning, even in a messy and concealed
perceptual field, has surely had a high survival value through the process of
evolution.

Leonardo observed the stimulating impact of eroding surfaces on the
imagination. Following an ancient Chinese instruction, he advised artists to
stare at a crumbling wall to gain inspiration:

THE FASCINATION OF ARCHITECTURAL RUINS

In their inherent tendency towards rationality, perfection and timelessness, buildings tend to remain outside our emotional and empathic reactions. The layering of traces of use, wear and time usually enriches the architectural image and invites our empathetic participation. Architectural ruins offer particularly potent images for nostalgic association and imagination, as if time and erosion would have undressed the structure of its disguise in utility and reason.

John Soane, The Soane House (Museum), 13 Lincoln's Inn Fields, London, 1792–1824. View of the Dome in 1811, Joseph Gandy, watercolour, 1370 × 800 mm.

Alvar Aalto, Experimental House, Muuratsalo, Finland, 1952–3. The brick and tile collage of the courtyard wall. The walls of the courtyard are made of bricks discarded at the contemporaneous construction site of the Säynätsalo Town Hall and special tiles from Aalto's other projects.

When you look at a wall spotted with stains or with a mixture of stones, if you have to devise some scene you may discover a resemblance of various landscapes … or, again, you may see battles and figures in action, or strange faces and costumes, or an endless variety of objects, which you could reduce to complete and well-drawn forms. And these appear on such walls promiscuously, like the sound of bells in whose jangle you may find any name or word you choose to imagine.[96]

The painterly images of Jackson Pollock and Henri Michaux are composed of accidental patches, splashes and shapes of ink or colour that are automatically interpreted as representational images or live characters in various dynamic activities, in accordance with Leonardo's suggestion. These subliminal, automatic interpretations also invoke our projected emotions: the suggested scene is either inviting or repulsive, pleasant or aggressive.

The image of a building has a similar stimulating power on our imagination. The quality and richness of an architectural image arises from the wealth of associative images and meanings that it evokes more than from the pure architectural gestalt itself. The image of a building instantly speaks of protection, familiarity and invitation, or of threat, strangeness and rejection. Such inherent characteristics of buildings and spaces are intuitively deployed by writers, filmmakers and other artists to create a distinct ambience for the event or human characters depicted in the story.

It is thought-provoking to notice that abandoned, damaged or destructed architectural settings often evoke richer and more emotional associations than perfected contemporary architecture. Even scenes of disaster or natural calamities, such as earthquakes, fires, explosions and train accidents, project curiously suggestive image qualities. Today's avant-garde architecture, such as Daniel Libeskind's museum designs, is often based on provocative images of dynamically destabilised structures which question the primacy of verticality and horizontality, the right angle and straight line, as well as established stylistic conventions (illustration, page 76, Daniel Libeskind, Extension to the Victoria and Albert Museum, London, UK, project). In their dynamic iconoclasm they make us recall countless historical images of architecture, as well as our stylistic expectations. The perfected architectural image is often a closed

and final image, whereas the scene of disturbance or destruction opens up a host of narratives reverberating with both past and future. Scenes of disaster reveal forces and events that are fundamentally beyond human control and, consequently, unexpected causalities and temporal sequences.

Peter Brook, the theatre director, deliberately demolished his theatre building Bouffes du Nord in Paris to create an associative and emotionally responsive space. 'A good space can't be neutral, for an impersonal sterility gives no food to the imagination. The Bouffes has the magic and the poetry of a ruin, and anyone who allowed themselves to be invaded by the atmosphere of a ruin knows strongly how the imagination is let loose,' he argues.[97]

In an essay on Peter Brook's destructive manipulation of architectural spaces for theatrical purposes, Andrew Todd writes:

> The walls engage time in a complex way. There is an after-echo of the original bourgeois music hall form, and this is rendered profound, even tragic, by the opening up of the layers of time on the walls. The top skin, which seals the imagination at a specific style or period, has been scorched away, so the walls exist in an indeterminate time, partway between cultural definition and eschatological dissolution. But this is no dead ruin: Brook has not been afraid to bash the place around a little more, breaking holes, putting in doors … One can also speak of another virtual patina the walls have acquired through the accruing memory of Brook's work in there.[98]

THE INTENTIONALLY DESTABILISED IMAGE

The normative language of architecture expresses stability, permanence and predictability. Violation, destruction and destabilisation of the architectural image introduces surprise, unpredictability and threat, and along with these new spatial and structural perceptions, new dimensions of emotion.

Matta-Clark's sculptural/architectural configurations violate the geometry of structural stability and permanence, whereas Libeskind's project presents a new spatial and structural concept that questions the age-old conventions of architecture.

Gordon Matta-Clark, *The Caribbean Orange*, 1978. Silver dye-bleach photograph. Museum of Fine Arts, Houston, Texas.

Daniel Libeskind, Extension to the Victoria and Albert Museum, London, UK, project, 1996.

The stains and signs of a dismantled building, left on the wall of the neighbouring house in Rainer Maria Rilke's *The Notebooks of Malte Laurids Brigge,* give a similar testimony of lives lived in the already absent rooms of the demolished house:

> There stood the middays and the sicknesses and the exhaled breath and the smoke of years, and the sweat that breaks out under armpits and makes clothes heavy, and the stale breath of mouths, and the fusel odor of sweltering feet. There stood the tang of urine and the burn of soot and the grey reek of potatoes, and the heavy, smooth stench of ageing grease. The sweet, lingering smell of neglected infants was there, and the fear-smell of children who go to school, and the sultriness out of the beds of nubile youths.[99]

Jean-Paul Sartre writes similarly about the fascinating emotional power of disaster and defeat:

> When the instruments are broken and unusable, when plans are blasted and effort is useless, the world appears with a childlike and terrible freshness without supports, without paths. It has a maximum reality because [...] defeat restores to things their individual reality [...] The defeat itself turns into salvation. For example, poetic language rises out of the ruins of prose.[100]

The ruined structure has ceased to play the role of a useful building; it is only a scaffolding for memory, a sheer melancholic presence without any utilitarian value. It has abandoned one-dimensional reason and rationality. The ruined, eroded, punctured, leaking and flooded buildings in Andrei Tarkovsky's films, such as *Stalker* and *Nostalghia*, as well as Gordon Matta-Clark's dramatically dissected buildings, expose entirely new spatial dynamics and tragic sentiments hidden behind the utilitarian face of architecture, and they exemplify the impact of destruction on our imagination and empathy (illustration, opposite, left).

Tarkovsky quotes Marcel Proust's phrase, 'raising the vast edifice of memories',[101] and regards this as the calling of film. We tend to project our feelings of empathy and compassion on scenes of damage and erosion, whereas perfected structures do not call for, or need, our sympathies as they present themselves self-sufficiently through their rational and instrumental values.

Images of time

What the past and the future have in common is our imagination, which conjures them [...] our imagination is rooted in our eschatological dread; the dread of thinking that we are without precedence or consequence. The stronger that dread, the more detailed our notion of antiquity and utopia.[102]

Joseph Brodsky, *Campidoglio*, 1994

Bachelard distinguishes the halted and vertical time of poetic imagery from the horizontal flow of daily life:

> Every real poem [...] contains the element of time stopped, time which does not obey the meter, time which we shall call *vertical* to distinguish it from ordinary time which seeps past horizontally along the wind and the waters of the stream. Whence this paradox, which we must note quite clearly: whereas prosodic time is horizontal, poetic time is vertical.[103] [Italics by Bachelard]

The experience of time and the sense of temporal duration and continuity have a seminal mental importance in architecture; we do not live only in space and place as we also inhabit time. Philosopher Karsten Harries points out the mental reality of time in architecture: 'Architecture is not only about domesticating space, it is also a deep defense against the terror of time. The language of beauty is essentially the language of the timeless reality.'[104]

Indeed, all the arts deal with and manipulate time. The experiential time in the arts can be compacted, accelerated, slowed down, reversed and halted. In architecture we can make a distinction between slow and fast architecture, between buildings that contain and hold time, and ones that evade or explode time. In a culture where time vanishes, or is exploded, as in our age of speed, the task of the arts seems to be to defend the comprehensibility of time, its experiential plasticity, tactility and slowness. Significantly, the speed of time is inversely related to our capacity of memory. Milan Kundera suggests that memorising is related to slowness, whereas speed results in forgetting.[105]

At the same time that great works of art are deeply engaged in the experiential dimension of time, they seem to neglect the progression of time altogether and resist its negative consequences. A cave painting that was painted in the deep darkness of a cave nearly 30,000 years ago, has the same vitality and image power as any of the art works conceived today. How does an artistic image maintain its freshness and its impact through endless time? When looking at a painting by Piero della Francesca or Johannes Vermeer, we can still feel the presence of the artist and imagine his hand guiding the brush in 'a universe [...] narrowed into what lies between each end of a paintbrush', as Randall Jarrell, the poet, points out.[106]

Paradoxically, the poetic image merges the dimensions of time and timelessness. The timeless reality of art is surely one of the greatest mysteries of our experiential and mental worlds. The experience of timelessness in art arises from the fact that the experience of art takes place in an imaginary world and mental reality, which are always re-created by the viewer; the experiential and emotive reality of the work is re-created in each successive encounter.

Bachelard writes in the 'Introduction to Chagall's Bible' about the magic of art in relation to time and contemporaneity:

> [W]ith his pencil in his hand, face to face with the darkness of the distant, so very distant past, surely Chagall is five thousand years old? His heart beats to a millennial rhythm. He is as old as what he sees [...] You will become caught up in one of the great dreams of temporality; you will come to know the musings of the millennia. Chagall will teach you, too, how to be five or six thousand years old.[107]

Historical environments contain benevolent and healing signs and traces of time, whereas contemporary architectural settings, with their artificial materials and industrialised techniques, do not usually strengthen the experience of a temporal continuum, a steady progression of time. The modern ideology aspires for a perpetual present tense and idolises impressions of youth and newness, and these ideals are also reflected in architecture. In today's culture, we can experience the simultaneous aspirations to halt and accelerate time, and these conflicting obsessions seem to create the time implosion that a number of post-modern philosophers have pointed out.

Illusionary image

As compared with the old world of experiential reality and causality, our technologised world contains ever more elements of illusion, immateriality and a-causality. This sense of dreamlike unreality is brought about by technologies that operate beyond the threshold of sensory perception and materials whose properties cannot any longer be detected by the senses. Glass is the ultimate material of this modern dream world and it is also the source of the illusory world of transparency, reflection and mirroring. It is a material of enticement and seduction, but reflective and mirroring surfaces also evoke estrangement and even fear. 'As a child, I felt before large mirrors that same horror of a spectral duplication or multiplication of reality [...] One of my persistent prayers to God and my guardian angel was that I not dream about mirrors,' writes Jorge Luis Borges of his fear of mirrors.[108] Mirrors create doubles, and doubling is experienced as disturbing and ominous. No wonder, the theme of the double is a frequent motif in literary and cinematic horror.

Seeing the world and oneself as a reflection may be stimulating, frightening or alienating. Literature, painting, photography and cinema offer us illuminating examples of the different meanings of these experiences. In Jean Cocteau's film *Orphée* (1949), the narcissistic protagonist disappears from this world through a mirror. In Andrei Tarkovsky's *Nostalghia* (1983), the protagonist-poet looks into a mirror, but is unexpectedly confronted with the image of the mad mathematician Domenico. Orson Welles' *The Lady from Shanghai* (1948) ends dramatically in a duel in a reflecting mirror cabinet, that annihilates the distinction between the real and the unreal, friend and foe, embodiment and ghostly reflection. Jacques Tati's *Play Time* (1969) is the ultimate cinematic parody of the varied confusions and frustrations evoked by the excessive use of glass in modern life.

In René Magritte's paintings, too, such as *Evening Falls* (1964) and *The Domain of Arnheim* (1949), the image of the world itself is shattered and the criteria of the real questioned. In artistic contexts, the ghostly perfection of the mirror is usually humanised by a scratched or corroded surface; the necrophilic perfection of the mirror is thus alleviated. The corroded mirrors in Tarkovsky's films exemplify this suppression and humanisation of threatening perfection. The current fashion to add silk-screened patterns or images on glass surfaces seems to be motivated as much by a desire to weaken the necrophilic impact of glass surfaces as by the attempt to reintroduce ornament in architecture.

Glass is usually seen as a symbol of democracy, equality and openness. Yet, a glass building may just as well invoke voyeurist control, corporate power, secrecy and even the loss of eyesight. New urban centres around the world frequently elicit this oppressive air of alienation, control and exclusion. Especially darkened, coloured and polarised glass surfaces tend to evoke this kind of negative experience, unless the material is used with great artistic distinction.

In the animistic world of architecture, buildings gesture and communicate by way of an unconscious bodily mimesis and identity through their forms, materiality, scale and details. Windows are the eyes of the house, and these eyes may be benevolent and inviting, or cruel and threatening. Broken windows are painfully experienced as violated and blinded eyes (illustration, page 126, Gordon Matta-Clark, *Window Blowout*). The eyes of the house may also appear attacked by some frightening illness, or they may turn blind; coloured and polarised glass often evokes the impression of a disturbing illness of the eye.

No technical ingenuity can erase these unconscious readings from our experiences of buildings, because our reading of the environment is biologically programmed; we are conditioned to identify unconsciously, in a split second, both hostility and benevolence. We animate our buildings unknowingly and we encounter them in the same way that we confront creatures of the living world.

Glass encourages experiences of illusion and dream. Its simultaneous transparency and opacity, reflection and fusion, presence and absence, transforms its surface into a dream landscape, an experiential collage. Indoors and outdoors, behind and in front, surface and depth, are all fused into simultaneous and enmeshed images.

Bachelard writes about a special category of poets, the 'water poets'.[109] Being a supercooled liquid, glass evokes images that are closely related to those of water. Consequently, we could also speak of 'glass poets'. Indeed, there are great poets among glass designers, artists, architects and engineers, all capable of imagining enchanting dreams of glass. They are able to express the multiple essences of the material, its simultaneous brittleness and malleability, hardness and fragility, immateriality and solidity, heaviness and weightlessness. In the basic alchemy of architecture there are two fundamental categories of matter: opaque matter and transparent matter. One creates separation, privacy and shadow, the other provides connectedness, visibility and light.

Beyond its utilitarian and technical qualities, glass is a material that has strong mythological, symbolic and utopian connotations. The desire for simultaneous visibility and invisibility, materiality and immateriality, presence and absence, is characteristic of the human psyche, and dreamlike images of houses and cathedrals of glass have persisted from the Middle Ages until the modern and post-modern eras. Through a succession of visionary projects, modern architecture has sought transparency, weightlessness and immateriality. These aspirations are epitomised by, for example, the great greenhouse structures of the 19th century, in particular the fabulous Crystal Palace in London for the 1851 Great Exhibition – in my view, the relatively most revolutionary and progressive building of all time, and an unsurpassed example of prefabrication and swift assembly. The crystalline structures of the German Expressionists Paul Scheerbart, Bruno Taut and Hans Scharoun prefigure Mies van der Rohe's 1920s all-glass tower projects and the utopian ambitions of the Russian Constructivists of the same period. The modern all-glass houses of Pierre Chareau, Paul Nelson, Mies van der Rohe and Philip Johnson exemplify this ideal, along with the countless all-glass buildings of today's Minimalist and High-Tech orientations.

A human existence caught within an invisible bubble of a transparent material has also been an enduring dream from Hieronymus Bosch's painterly vision of 'Paradise' in the early 15th century to Reyner Banham's environmental bubble of the late 1960s. In Banham's influential essay of the late 1960s entitled 'A Home Is Not a House', he argued that mechanical technology is gradually becoming more important than the traditional material components of architecture, and that the house will eventually turn into a purely mechanical device for environmental control. With this vision, Banham implied the end of architecture as traditionally conceived. In his view, our understanding of architecture and its aesthetics need to be radically re-evaluated as a consequence of the development towards ever more refined and efficient technology and gradually increasing invisibility.[110] We can therefore appropriately speak of 'an invisible architecture'. In the utopian atmosphere of the 1960s, Hans Hollein actually proposed an environmental pill that would project the mental experiences of various architectural conditions by means of chemical induction. Buckminster Fuller, Yona Friedman, Frei Otto and many others expanded the idea of an invisible environmental shelter to the grand scale of the metropolis and the landscape. Many of these futuristic images were, in fact, realised in the projects of Nicholas Grimshaw, Norman Foster, Richard Rogers and others in the 1970s and 80s.

André Breton brings the modern image of the glass house to its ultimate limit: '... I continue to inhabit my glass house, where one can see at every hour who is coming to visit me, where everything that is suspended from the ceilings and the walls holds on as if by enchantment, where I rest at night on a bed of glass with glass sheets, where who I am will appear to me, sooner or later, engraved by a diamond'. [111]

The iconic image

The notion 'icon' refers initially to Byzantine and Orthodox religious paintings of Christ and saints. This painting tradition did not aspire to a deliberately individual artistic expression as icons were painted following strict rules of a prevailing representational canon.

In modern language, the use of the notion has been expanded to denote any authoritative image, object or even personality. 'Iconic work' and 'iconic image' usually refer to works of art or singular images which have become authoritatively approved by the artistic culture or popularly idolised, or are considered seminal representatives of a distinct genre of art. Vincent Van Gogh's *Sunflowers* (1888), Pablo Picasso's *Guernica* (1937), Piet Mondrian's *Broadway Boogie Woogie* (1942/43), and Andy Warhol's *Turquoise Marilyn* (1962), for instance, would probably be accepted as painterly icons in the public eye.

Similarly, iconic works in architecture are buildings or projects which exemplify authoritatively and memorably a distinct formal approach. Gerrit Rietveld's Schröder House (1924) in Utrecht, Pierre Chareau's Maison de Verre (1929) in Paris, Konstantin Melnikov's House (1929) in Moscow, Le Corbusier's Villa Savoye (1928–9) in Poissy, Frank Lloyd Wright's Fallingwater House (1936) in Bear Run, Pennsylvania and Mies van der Rohe's Farnsworth House (1946–51) in Plano, Illinois can be unreservedly listed as iconic houses in modern architectural history. They are all concentrations of a powerful conceptual idea and a striking and memorable formal image, and they have had a considerable influence on the course of architecture. Each one of them represents a unique 'architectural species' and they have all given rise to countless adaptations, albeit with decisively weaker image power than the originals. No doubt, a few dozen other houses, such as RM Schindler's Schindler House (1921–2) in Los Angeles, Curzio Malaparte's Casa Malaparte (1930–40) in Capri, Angelo Invernizzi and Ettore Fagiouli's Villa Girasole (1929–35) in Marcellise, Verona, and Charles Eames' Eames House (1945–9) in Santa Monica, California, would also qualify as iconic houses.

An iconic image crystallises and perfects an idea to the point that no significant improvement can be expected within that particular concept. The iconic image simultaneously opens and closes a specific line of thought and development.

Like the original religious icon paintings, an iconic piece of architecture radiates a special aura and sense of significance and authority. Due to its ambience of perfection and absoluteness, an iconic image may even obtain an otherworldly aura of sacredness. The *Black Square* of Kazimir Malevich (1913) and Ad Reinhardt's almost black paintings of the 1960s, with a vague figure that appears only after a prolonged gaze, have a distinct air of religious icons regardless of the absence of narrative, symbolic or figural subject matter. Iconic buildings, also, exude an imposing or awe-inspiring air, as the material work invites one's full awareness into an imaginative, spiritual reality.

The epic image

The innate experiential richness of profound artistic images gives rise to epic readings; a verse turns into a story of human destiny, and the narrative of an entire era. A painted abstraction, such as Mark Rothko's dark paintings in the Rothko Chapel in Houston, guides the onlooker to the very borderline between life and death, being and non-being. Walker Evans' *Farmer's Kitchen* (1936) is a simple photograph of a poor farm worker's wooden kitchen seen through a doorway, but the metal washing bowl, the adjacent white linen towel, oil lamp on the kitchen table and other household objects turn the picture into a heart-rending image of domesticity, cleanliness and the sacredness of simple life. Also, a masterful piece of architecture, such as Alvar Aalto's Villa Mairea (illustration, opposite, right), turns into an epic narrative of cultural history and life, nature and artifice, utility and beauty, and it offers an empowering promise of a more humane future. This house is not an ordinary tectonic Modernist structure; it fuses irreconcilable imageries into a symphonic whole. This architectural imagery is further enriched and deepened by images of modern art. Already, upon arrival, the house presents an extraordinarily cordial welcome and gives a silent promise to take good care of the visitor.

In his well-known reading of the image of Vincent van Gogh's *A Pair of Shoes* (1886) (illustration, opposite, left), Martin Heidegger interprets a pair of worn-out shoes of a Dutch farmer's wife as an epic narrative that unfolds from these worthless objects before the beholder's very eyes. The fact that the artist painted this canvas in Paris, apparently using his own pair of shoes as

THE EPIC IMAGE IN ART AND ARCHITECTURE

Artistic images are condensations of experiences and meanings. They don't merely depict objects as their subject matter or organise practicalities of human activities; paintings and buildings are comprehensive images of culture and life. A pair of worn-out shoes can tell an epic story of toilsome farm life, while a house is an inexhaustible narrative of its era and a way of life with its daily routines and spiritual aspirations.

Vincent Van Gogh, *A Pair of Shoes*, 1886. Van Gogh Museum, Amsterdam, The Netherlands.

Martin Heidegger's literary description of the pair of peasant shoes reveals the epic scope of the artist's depiction of ordinary objects.

Alvar Aalto, Villa Mairea, Noormarkku, Finland, 1938–9. South facade.

Aalto's masterpiece is one of the most poetic and experientially rich residential designs of the 20th century.

the model, does not diminish the poetic suggestiveness of the philosopher's words. This insignificant pair of footwear represents an entire way of burdened life, captured and reflected in the battered image:

> From the dark opening of the worn insides of the shoes the toilsome tread of the worker stares forth. In the stiffly rugged heaviness of the shoes there is the accumulated tenacity of her slow trudge through the far-spreading and ever-uniform furrows of the field swept by raw wind. On the leather lie the dampness and richness of the soil. Under the soles slides the loneliness of the field-path as evening falls. In the shoes vibrates the silent call of the earth. Its quiet gift of the ripening grain and its unexplained self-refusal in the fallow desolation of the wintry field. This equipment is pervaded by uncomplaining worry as to the certainty of bread, the wordless joy of having once more withstood want, the trembling before the impending childbed and shivering at the surrounding menace of death.[112]

Rainer Maria Rilke provides the most astonishing record of what it takes to create a profound artistic image, a single line of verse. Poetic insightfulness is not merely a matter of verbal, painterly or spatial inventiveness. In the poet's view, it calls for a deep understanding and love of life.

> … [V]erses are not, as people imagine, simply feelings … they are experiences. For the sake of a single verse, one must see many cities, men and things, one must know the animals, one must feel how the birds fly and know the gesture with which the little flowers open in the morning.[113]

The poet continues the list of experiences that constitute the mental ground for the gradual emergence of a poetic image dramatically and seemingly endlessly:

> … One must have memories of many nights of love, none of which was like the others, of the screams of women in labor, and of light, white, sleeping women in childbed, closing again. But one must also have been beside the dying, must have sat beside the dead in the room with the open window and the fitful noises.[114]

But all these encounters of the full drama of life are not yet an adequate ground for the poet's work; the creative spark is embedded in the internalised memories of these experiences that have become part of the poet's very being:

> And still it is not yet enough to have memories. One must be able to forget them when they are many and one must have the great patience to wait until they come again. For it is not yet the memories themselves. Not till they have turned to blood within us, to glance and gesture, nameless and no longer to be distinguished from ourselves – not till then can it happen that in a most rare hour the first word of verse arises in their midst and goes forth from them.[115]

The poet's description of the experiential and emotional prerequisites for the emergence of a line of verse reveals monumentally the epic scope and depth of true artistic imagery. No one who has read Rilke's description can think of art as mere aesthetic or formal invention.

Architectural images similarly have an epic scope, as they are images of both lived and potential life. Profound houses, such as the masterpieces of residential architecture in history and today, offer benevolent images of domesticity, rootedness and well-being. They are invitations to a dignified life. Even deserted houses project stories of true life with messages of bliss and sorrow, security and fear, affection and abandonment. Through their imagery as cultural institutions, museum buildings project images of cultural heritage and continuity, theatre and opera buildings suggest imaginary worlds of fantasy and festive social gatherings, whereas churches concretise the metaphysical dimensions of life and the consoling realm of faith. Entire cities are lived metaphors that organise and guide myriad activities of daily life, direct our thoughts and emotions, and make us know who we are.

Poetic images as worlds

ARTISTIC IMAGES AS
WORLDS

Great artistic works create
their own microcosm or
universe. They are not
merely depictions of selected
objects, or resolutions to a
specific design task; they
possess their own fields of
gravity, orbits and sources
of light. They represent
simultaneously a beginning
and an end, a question and
the answer. Profound artistic
images make us look at the
world anew and experience
our own condition with a
heightened intensity.

Giorgio Morandi, *Still Life*, c
1952. Oil on canvas. Private
collection.

The tiny still life projects a
metaphysical question on a
monumental scale.

Mies van der Rohe, House
for Edith Farnsworth, Plano,
Illinois, 1946–51.

The house is a perfectly
aestheticised and complete
object, a metaphor of the
world.

Profound artistic images are not singular pictures, snapshots, confined views, aspects or details; they are entire worlds. They are complete microcosms rather than depictions of isolated and framed events, figures or still lifes. Andrei Tarkovsky makes a statement to this effect on the essence of the cinematic image: 'In a word, the image is not a certain meaning expressed by the director, but an entire world reflected as in a drop of water.'[116]

No city of a meaningful film ends at the edge of the frame, as the space spreads around interminably in the consciousness of the viewer, in the manner of real cities. In fact, a literary or cinematic city does not even cease to exist when the book or film is over, as the imaginary city has been transferred into the mind and memory of the beholder, and life continues within its imagined walls.

The compressed still lifes of Giorgio Morandi (illustration, below, left) do not only depict a few timid objects on a table top, seeking protection from each other; these minute paintings are complete microcosms. Instead of being mere pictures, these overtly humble paintings are powerful metaphysical propositions and philosophical meditations on existence and being, silence and solitude. Instead of portraying this or that household object, they demonstrate the very enigma of being. 'How is it that things exist in this world?,' those simultaneously tiny and monumental paintings seem to ask.

It is the microcosmic fullness and completeness of artistic images that gives them their authority and inexhaustible content. Through our capacity

for emotive identification, the imaginary obtains the authority of the real and the real turns into a mystery. Poetic images branch out, fuse with and metamorphose into other images. Profound images – even the most condensed and 'abstract' of them – are not stable, as they have their inner dynamic life. Everything that is alive, biologically or mentally, seeks interaction and dialogue with other things.

At the very end of his last film *Beyond the Clouds* (1994), Michelangelo Antonioni, the architect of cinematic images, expresses this complexity and enigmatic richness of artistic imagery through the words of the protagonist, a photographer (played by John Malkovich): 'But we know that behind every image revealed, there is another image, more faithful to reality, and in the back of that image there is another, and yet another behind the last one, and so on, up to the true image of the absolute mysterious reality that no-one will ever see.'[117] These successively associative images reveal their layered experiential and mental realities in the way that an ancient Egyptian mummy or a Russian doll gradually reveals its successively hidden images.

Each time one views again a great film, re-reads a fine novel, looks repeatedly at a masterpiece of painting, or revisits an architectural classic, the more one discovers. The poetic image takes us to the moment of the first innocent, but immensely potent encounter. A profound piece of architecture is always novel and unexpected, no matter how many times one revisits it, as it lives and reflects life itself. Timeless freshness, a kind of untouchable newness, is a quality of the greatest of artistic images, including those of architecture.

References

1 Andrei Tarkovsky, *Sculpting in Time – Reflections on the Cinema*, Bodley Head (London), 1986, p 21.

2 Robert Graves, *The White Goddess*, Farrar, Straus and Giroux (New York), 1948, p 24.

3 Gaston Bachelard, *The Right to Dream*, Dallas Institute Publications (Dallas, TX), 1988, p 173.

4 Jorge Luis Borges, foreword to *Obra Poetica, Selected Poems 1923–1967*, as quoted in Sören Thurell, *The Shadow of a Thought: The Janus Concept of Architecture*, School of Architecture, The Royal Institute of Technology (Stockholm), 1989, p 2.

5 Referred to in Arnold H Modell, *Imagination and the Meaningful Brain*, MIT Press (Cambridge, MA and London, UK), 2006, p 12.

6 Elaine Scarry, 'On Solidity', *Dreaming by the Book*, Princeton University Press (Princeton, NJ), 2001, pp 10–30.

7 Scarry, *Dreaming by the Book*, 2001, p 30.

8 Bohumil Hrabal, *Too Loud a Solitude*, Harcourt, Inc (San Diego, New York, London), 1990, p 1.

9 Charles Tomlinson, 'The Poet as Painter', in JM McClatchy, editor, *Poets on Painters*, University of California Press (Berkeley, Los Angeles, London), 1990, p 280.

10 Maurice Merleau-Ponty, as quoted in Tomlinson, 'The Poet as Painter', in McClatchy, *Poets on Painters*, 1990, p 275.

11 For the bio-historical approach, see: Jay Appleton, *The Experience of Landscape*, John Wiley & Sons (London), 1996; Edward O Wilson, *Biophilia: The Human Bond with Other Species*, Harvard University Press (Cambridge, MA and London, UK), 1984; Grant Hildebrand, *The Wright Space: Pattern & Meaning in Frank Lloyd Wright's Houses*, University of Washington Press (Seattle), 1991; Grant Hildebrand, *Origins of Architectural Pleasure*, University of California Press (Berkeley, Los Angeles, London), 1999.

12 Semir Zeki, *Inner Vision: An Exploration of Art and the Brain*, Oxford University Press (Oxford), 1999, and John Onians, *Neuroarthistory: From Aristotle and Pliny to Baxandall and Zeki*, Yale University Press (New Haven and London), 2007.

13 As quoted in Eric Shanes, *Constantin Brancusi*, Abbeville Press (New York), 1989, p 67.

14 Tomlinson, 'The Poet as Painter', in McClatchy, *Poets on Painters*, 1990, p 284.

15 Gaston Bachelard, *The Philosophy of No: A Philosophy of the New Scientific Mind*, Orion Press (New York), 1968, pp 9–10.

16 Ibid. p 16.

17 Gaston Bachelard, *Water and Dreams: An Essay On the Imagination of Matter*, Pegasus Foundation (Dallas, TX), 1999, p 50.

18 'The Relationship Between Architecture, Painting and Sculpture', interview by Karl Fleig for *Alvar Aalto, Synopsis*, Birkhäuser Verlag (Basel), 1970. Republished in *Alvar Aalto in His Own Words*, edited and annotated by Göran Schildt, Otava Publishing Company (Helsinki), 1997, pp 267–8.

19 Bachelard, *Water and Dreams*, 1999, p VII.

20 Ibid. p 1.

21 Ibid. p 22.

22 As quoted in Mohsen Mostafavi and David Leatherbarrow, *On Weathering*, MIT Press (Cambridge, MA), 1993, p 76.

23 Le Corbusier, *L'art décoratif d'aujourd'hui*, Editions G. Grès et Cie (Paris), 1925, p 192.

24 Bachelard, *Water and Dreams,* 1999, p 22.

25 Maurice Merleau-Ponty, 'Cezanne's Doubt', in Maurice Merleau-Ponty, *Sense and Non-Sense*, Northwestern University Press (Evanston, IL), 1964, p 12.

26 Paul Valéry, 'Eupalinos, or the Architect', *Paul Valéry Dialogues*, Pantheon Books (New York), 1956, p 70.

27 Gaston Bachelard, *The Psychoanalysis of Fire*, Beacon Press (Boston), 1968; and, Bachelard, *Water and Dreams,* 1999, third printing.

28 Gaston Bachelard, *The Flame of a Candle*, Dallas Institute Publications (Dallas, TX), 1988, p 1.

29 Bachelard, *Water and Dreams,* 1999, p 5.

30 Ibid. p 15.

31 Joseph Brodsky, *Watermark*, Penguin Books (London), 1992, pp 43 and 134.

32 Adrian Stokes, 'Prologue: at Venice', *The Critical Writings of Adrian Stokes*, Vol II, Thames & Hudson (Plymouth), 1978, p 88.

33 Jacques Aumont, *The Image*, British Film Institute (London), 1997, p 199.

34 Anton Ehrenzweig, *The Hidden Order of Art*, Paladin (Frogmore, St Albans), 1973, p 14.

35 Arthur Koestler, *The Act of Creation*, Hutchinson (London), 1964, p 158.

36 Ibid.

37 Ibid. p 180.

38 Merleau-Ponty, *Sense and Non-Sense*, 1964, p 48.

39 Gaston Bachelard, *The Poetics of Reverie*, Beacon Press (Boston), 1971, p 6.
40 Maurice Merleau-Ponty, *Phenomenology of Perception*, Routledge and Kegan Paul (London), 1962, p 235.
41 John Dewey, *Art As Experience*, Perigee Books (New York), 1980.
42 Ibid. pp 122–4.
43 As referred to in Bernard Berenson, *Aesthetics and History*, Pantheon Books (New York), 1948, pp 66–70.
44 Oliver Sacks, 'The Mind's Eye: What the Blind See', in *Empire of the Senses*, edited by David Howes, Berg Publishers (Oxford), 2005, p 33.
45 Jacques Lusseyran (1987), as referred to by Sacks, p 36.
46 C Castoriadis (1997), as referred to by Modell, *Imagination and the Meaningful Brain*, 2006, p 209.
47 Walt Whitman, 'Faith Poem', poem 20, *Leaves of Grass,* 1856.
48 Anton Ehrenzweig, *The Hidden Order of Art*, University of California Press (Berkeley and Los Angeles), 1967, p 129.
49 Ibid. p 132.
50 Catalogue of Brancusi Exhibition, Brummer Gallery, New York, 1926. As republished in Eric Shanes, *Constantin Brancusi*. Abbeville Press (New York), 1989, p 106.
51 Jan Vrijman, 'Filmmakers Spacemakers', *The Berlage Papers* 11 (January 1994).
52 Walter Benjamin, 'The Work of Art in the Age of Mechanical Reproduction', *Illuminations*, Hannah Arendt, editor, Schocken Books (New York), 1968.
53 Bachelard, *The Flame of a Candle,* 1988, p 34.
54 Carl G Jung, 'Approaching the Unconscious', *Man and His Symbols*, edited by Carl G Jung et al, Laurel (New York), 1968, p 87.
55 Jung, *Man and His Symbols*, 1968, p 57.
56 Sinclair Gauldie,

Architecture, Oxford University Press (London and New York), 1969, as quoted in Juan Pablo Bonta, *Architecture and its Interpretation: A Study of Expressive Systems in Architecture*, Lund Humphries Publishers (London), 1979, p 31.
57 Gaston Bachelard, *The Poetics of Space*, Beacon Press (Boston), 1969, p 6.
58 Adrian Stokes, 'Smooth and Rough', as quoted in Colin St John Wilson, 'Alvar Aalto and the State of Modernism' in *Alvar Aalto vs the Modern Movement*, Kirmo Mikkola, editor, Rakennuskirja Oy (Helsinki), 1981, p 114.
59 Aniela Jaffé, 'Symbolism in the Visual Arts', in Jung et al, *Man and His Symbols,* 1968, pp 255–322.
60 Fourfold symbolism is discussed in detail in: Anna C Esmeijer, *Divina Quaternitas: A Preliminary Study in the Method and Application of Visual Exegesis*, Van Gorcum (Assen), 1978.
61 Sol LeWitt, 'The Cube', *Art in America* (New York), summer 1966.
62 Andrei Tarkovsky, *Sculpting in Time – Reflections on the Cinema*, Bodley Head (London), 1986, p 212–13.
63 Jaffé, as quoted in Jung, *Man and His Symbols*, 1968, pp 268–9.
64 The story of the founding of Rome as well as other myths of the founding rituals of cities in the Old World are presented in Joseph Rykwert, *The Idea of a Town: the Anthropology of Urban Form in Rome, Italy and the Ancient World*, MIT Press (Cambridge, MA), 1988.
65 The complex symbolism of the Dogon tribe is discussed in a fascinating book: Marcel Griaule, *Conversations with Ogotemmêli: An Introduction to Dogon Religious Ideas*, Oxford University Press (London), 1965.
66 Scarry, *Dreaming by the Book*, 2001, p 5.
67 As quoted in Richard

Kearney, *The Wake of Imagination*, Routledge (London), 1994, p 230.
68 Guy Davenport, 'Balthus', in McClatchy, *Poets on Painters*, 1990, p 235.
69 Gaston Bachelard, *The Poetics of Space* (1958), Beacon Press (Boston), 1969, p XIX.
70 Colin St John Wilson, 'Architecture – Public Good and Private Necessity', *RIBA Journal*, March 1979.
71 Jaffé, as quoted in Jung, *Man and His Symbols*, 1968, p 308.
72 Ehrenzweig, *The Hidden Order of Art*, 1967, pp 21–31.
73 Ibid. pp 32–46.
74 Alvar Aalto, 'Art and Technology', in *Alvar Aalto in His Own Words*, 1997, p 174.
75 Modell, *Imagination and the Meaningful Brain*, 2006, p XII. Modell's argument is based on the views of Mark Johnson and George Lakoff on how meaning arises in the unconscious mind.
76 Gaston Bachelard, *On Poetic Imagination and Reverie*, selected, translated and introduced by Colette Gaudin, Spring Publications (Dallas, TX), 1998, p XXXVII.
77 As quoted in Modell, *Imagination and the Meaningful Brain*, 2006, p 117.
78 Aristotle, *Poetics*, JM Dent & Sons (London), 1934, p 45.
79 Iris Murdoch, *The Sovereignty of Good*, Routledge & Kegan Paul (London), 1970, as quoted in Modell, p 26.
80 As quoted in Modell, *Imagination and the Meaningful Brain*, 2006, p 1.
81 George Lakoff and Mark Johnson, *Metaphors We Live By*, University of Chicago (Chicago), 1980.
82 Modell, *Imagination and the Meaningful Brain*, 2006, p 32.
83 Ibid. p 27.
84 Bachelard, *The Poetics of Space*, 1969, p XXX.
85 Nurur Rahman Khan, 'The Assembly Building', *The Assembly Building*, Department of Architecture, The University

of Asia Pacific (Dhaka), 2001, p 1.

86 Khaleed Ashraf, as quoted in Khan, *The Assembly Building*, 2001, p 6.

87 Vittorio Gallese, as quoted in Modell, *Imagination and the Meaningful Brain*, 2006, p 121.

Vittorio Gallese and Giacomo Rizzolatti codiscovered mirror neurons. Their experiments show that our brains resonate with the other's feelings in the same way as we resonate with the other's intentional actions. Their studies support the contention that empathy originates in the body and these processes are unconscious.

Gallese explains further the neural mechanism which makes us unconsciously simulate actions that we observe: 'Whenever we are looking at someone performing an action, beside the activation of various visual areas, there is a concurrent activation of the motor circuits that are recruited when we ourselves perform that action [...] Our motor system becomes active as if we were executing the very same action that we are observing [...] Action observation implies action simulation [...] our motor system starts to covertly simulate the actions of the observed agent.'

Vittorio Gallese, 'The "Shared Manifold" Hypothesis: from Mirror Neurons to Empathy', *Journal of Consciousness Studies* 8: 2001, pp 33–50. As quoted in Shaun Gallagher and Dan Zahavi, *The Phenomenological Mind*, Routledge (London and New York), 2008, p 178.

88 As quoted in Modell, *Imagination and the Meaningful Brain*, 2006, p 183.

89 Richard Kearney, *Poetics of Imagining: From Husserl to Lyotard*, Harper Collins Academic (London), 1991, p 59.

90 Ibid. p 70.

91 As quoted in Wallace Stevens, 'Two Prefaces. Gloire du long désir, Idées', *Paul Valéry Dialogues*, Pantheon Books (New York), 1956, p XIII.

92 As quoted in Modell, *Imagination and the Meaningful Brain*, 2006, p 184.

93 Modell, *Imagination and the Meaningful Brain*, 2006, p 187.

94 Ibid. p 185.

95 John Soane, 'Crude Hints towards an History of my House in Lincoln's Inn Fields', in *Visions of Ruin: Architectural Fantasies & Designs for Garden Follies*, The Soane Gallery (London), 1999.

96 As quoted in Robert Hughes, *The Shock of the New: Art and the Century of Change*, Thames & Hudson (London), 1980, p 225.

97 Andrew Todd and Jean-Guy Lecat, *The Open Circle: Peter Brook's Theatre Environments*, Palgrave MacMillan (New York), 2003, p 25.

98 Andrew Todd, 'Learning From Peter Brook's Work on Theatre Space', manuscript 25, September 1999, p 4.

99 Rainer Maria Rilke, *The Notebooks of Malte Laurids Brigge*, WW Norton & Company (New York and London), 1992, pp 47–8.

100 Jean-Paul Sartre, *What is Literature?*, Peter Smith (Gloucester, MA), 1978, p 30.

101 Tarkovsky, *Sculpting in Time*, 1986, p 59.

102 Joseph Brodsky, 'Homage to Marcus Aurelius', *Campidoglio*, Random House (New York), 1994, p 31.

103 Gaston Bachelard, *The Right to Dream*, 1988, p 173.

104 Karsten Harries, 'Building and the Terror of Time', *Perspecta, The Yale Architectural Journal*, issue 19, MIT Press (Cambridge, MA), 1982, as quoted in David Harvey, *The Condition of Postmodernity*, Blackwell (Cambridge, MA), 1992, p 206.

105 Milan Kundera, *Slowness*, Harper Collins Publishers (New York), 1996, p 39.

106 Randall Jarrell, 'Against Abstract Expressionism', in *Poets on Painters*, p 189.

107 Gaston Bachelard, *The Right to Dream*, Dallas Institute Publications (Dallas, TX), 1971, p 10.

108 Jorge Luis Borges, 'The Draped Mirrors', in Jorge Luis Borges, *Dreamtigers*, University of Texas Press (Austin), 2001, p 27.

109 Bachelard, *Water and Dreams,* Pegasus Foundation (Dallas, TX), 1983, p 5.

110 Reyner Banham, 'A Home Is Not a House', *Art in America* (April 1965), pp 109–18.

111 André Breton, *Nadja,* as quoted in Anthony Vidler, *The Architectural Uncanny*, MIT Press (London), 1999, p 218.

112 Martin Heidegger, 'The Origin of the Work of Art', *Basic Writings*, Harper & Row (New York), 1977, p 163.

113 Rilke, *The Notebooks of Malte Laurids Brigge*, 1992, p 26.

114 Ibid.

115 Ibid. p 26–7.

116 Tarkovsky, *Sculpting in Time*, 1986, p 110.

117 Michelangelo Antonioni, *Beyond the Clouds* (1994). The protagonist's final words on the sound track.

4

The anatomy of the poetic image

The question is: by what miracle is a writer able to incite us to bring forth mental images that resemble in their quality not our own daydreaming but our own (much more freely practiced) perceptual acts?[1]

Elaine Scarry, *Dreaming by the Book*, 1999

Imagination is not, as its etymology would suggest, the faculty of forming images of reality; it is rather the faculty of forming images which go beyond reality, which sing reality. It is a superhuman quality.[2]

Gaston Bachelard, *Water and Dreams*, 1999

The poetic image exists simultaneously in two realities: the physical reality of perception and the 'unreal' realm of imagination. The hypnotic power of great artistic works derives from this simultaneity that short-circuits rational understanding. Artistic images also possess a generality and specificity at the same time: generality in terms of arising from human existential experience, and specificity in the sense of articulating experiential and mental phenomena that are ontologically specific to each art form.

Instead of being mere aestheticisation, true artistic works represent particular modes of thinking specific to them. The artistic image is engaged in time both through articulating deep and timeless mental phenomena, and by manipulating our experience of the temporal dimension.

The dual existence of the poetic image

The mental or lived image is a central notion in all the arts, although neither artists nor theorists often allude to it. When mentioned, the word 'image' usually refers to purely perceptual or visual phenomena. However, the image is the experiential entity, the synthetic perceptual, cognitive and emotional singularity of the artistic work that is perceived, embodied and remembered. It is, at the same time, the identity of the work, the very core of its impact and its emotional and existential meaning. The poetic image is a distinct imaginary experiential entity with its cohesive identity, anatomy and essence. The poetic image redirects and focuses the viewer/listener/reader/occupant's attention and gives rise to an altered state of consciousness, which evokes an imaginary dimension, an imaginative world.

As was already pointed out in Chapter 3 in 'The Reality and Unreality of the Artistic Image', there is a fundamental dualism in the artistic image itself. An artistic work exists simultaneously in two realities: the physical reality of its material essence and processes of execution and making, and in the imaginary reality of its artistic image, suggestion and expressive structure. As a consequence, a work of art is simultaneously here and elsewhere, in the physical and in an imaginary world. A painting is paint on canvas, on the one hand, and an imaginary picture, suggestion, event or microcosm, on the other. A sculpture is similarly a piece of stone, bronze or wood, and a plastic image. A piece of music is simultaneously sound with its technical performance and an emotive and mental space in its self-contained and complete musical world. A building is a structure of utility, matter and construction, as well as an imaginary spatiotemporal metaphor for a better world. Artistic and architectural works exist thus in the realms of physics and metaphysics, reality and fiction, construction and image, use and desire, all at the same time.

In the perception of the poetic image, the material existence of the work is suppressed as the experience of the imaginary world takes over. As we are experiencing an artistic work, our awareness is suspended and shifting between these two realities, and the tension between the two awarenesses charges the work with a magical power. The magic 'aura' of the work arises from this very duality and tension as much as from its recognisable subject matter and sense of authority deriving from a masterly execution.

In the mental internalisation of and identification with an image, the fact whether we are dealing with a unique and singular piece of art, or a mass-produced reproduction, makes no fundamental difference. In their physical and cultural roles images naturally vary, and an original painting by a master, for instance, reflects faculties of authenticity, detail and value that do not exist in a reproduction. But in any case, through the experience, the image turns into an imaginative reality. Excessive reproduction and presence of an image tends to weaken and render banal its effect, although the mysterious quality of great works is exactly their capacity to maintain their aura and spell.

Through their cultural exploitation, iconic works of art and architecture tend to turn into signs that have lost their authenticity and seductive power. The

All artistic works are
suspended between their
material existence and the
imaginary image that they
evoke. The hypnotic power of
the work arises from this dual
existence. In the case that
the impression of material
and execution dominate, the
work appears crude and raw,
whereas the piece appears
sentimental and kitsch when
the illusion of the image
is not counterbalanced by
traces of the real world such
as materiality, or the evidence
of its making.

François Gérard, Psyche
receives the first kiss of love,
Cupid and Psyche, 1798. Oil
on canvas, 186 × 132 cm.
Museum of the Louvre, Paris.

The high illusionism of the
painted mythological scene
tends to create a feeling of
kitsch.

Kain Tapper, Feeling of
Nature II, 1981. Birch and
pine wood, 105 × 80 × 80
cm. Orion Company, Espoo.

The minimal articulation of
the sculpted form appears as
a potential and suggestive
image rather than any
finite gestalt or meaning.
It is a representation of an
image concealed in matter,
reminiscent of Michelangelo's
slaves.

pyramids can be experienced merely as symbols of ancient Egypt, and the
Opera House by Jørn Utzon as a symbol of Sydney and an example of uniquely
creative architecture. Tourism and cultural industry turn masterpieces of art
into concepts and historical symbols.

The shift from perceptual to imaginative consciousness determines the
character and quality of the work. When the imaginary realm overwhelms,
the work appears sentimental or kitsch as our mental awareness glides too
easily into the suggested illusion (illustration, opposite, left). Vice versa, when
the reality of matter or execution dominates, the work tends to appear crude
and unarticulated, and it seems incapable of evoking a credible imaginary
world (illustration, opposite, right). A powerful work always maintains a
tension between the two realities. A great painting keeps us fully aware that
the image is a physical and real object and a mental suggestion at the same
time. In a fine theatre performance we remain conscious of the reality of
the play, whereas a flawed performance makes us painfully conscious of the
reality of naive acting only. An architectural work is simultaneously taken as a
practical context of action and a mental metaphor of space, structure, matter
and light; the building affects simultaneously our behaviour, imagination and
emotions.

The comparison of Michelangelo's two Pietàs illuminates this duality. The Pietà
that Michelangelo executed at the age of 23 is a virtuoso example of sculptural
representation by a young genius. However, his Rondanini Pietà (1552–64)
in Castello Sforzesco in Milan, the last piece that Michelangelo worked on six
days before his death in 1564, appears crude and unfinished. Upon a deeper
comparison, however, the marble of the first piece seems to turn too easily
into flesh, whereas the latter piece is dramatically and tragically a piece of
stone (the sculptor used an unfinished sculpture as his material for the work
and there is an extra human arm, next to the two figures, that the artist did
not eliminate) and a coarsely but tenderly crafted biblical image at the same
time. The first piece calls for our admiration and awe, whereas the deep tragic
ambience of the Rondanini Pietà brings tears to our eyes.

The artist must keep his/her role as the creator of the imaginary reality apart
from that of the onlooker/reader's. In his short story The Duel, Jorge Luis
Borges tells the shocking story of two Argentinian gauchos who had hated
each other all their lives. The two men are taken prisoner in a civil war, and
made to compete in running with their throats cut. Borges explains that the
writer must be 'always tuning things down'. 'Reality is not always probable,

or likely. But if you're writing a story, you have to make it as plausible as you can, because otherwise the reader's imagination will reject it,' he confesses.[3] 'In order to make it [the story] horrifying I left the horror to the reader's imagination. I couldn't very well say, "what an awful thing happened", or "this story is very gruesome", because I would make a fool of myself. The kind of thing must be left to readers, not to writers. Otherwise, the whole thing goes to pieces.'[4]

A masterful artist makes the viewer/reader experience, see and think other things than what he/she is actually being exposed to. The lines of Piet Mondrian's diagonal paintings (for example, *Lozenge Composition with Four Lines and Grey*, 1926, the Museum of Modern Art, New York), that meet beyond the edges of the canvas, make us aware of the space outside the painting. In the penultimate scene of Antonioni's *The Passenger* (1974), the protagonist (played by Jack Nicholson) is murdered behind our back as we are watching arbitrary and insignificant incidents of everyday life through a window open to a courtyard. Fritz Lang comments on the invisible contents of his film *M* (1931): 'There is no violence in my film *M*, or when there is, it occurs behind the scenes, as it were. Let's take an example. You will remember the sequence where a little girl is murdered. All you see is a ball rolling and then stopping. Then a balloon flying off and getting caught in some telephone wires … The violence is in your mind.'[5]

In architecture, likewise, the artistic motifs should not be excessive or overly dramatised, because our 'imagination will reject them', as Borges

advises writers. The strategies of holding back and understatement have a heightened value in architecture. If it aspires to a permanent mental impact, an architectural work has to engage our personal and active imagination; even an architectural narrative has to be left incomplete and open-ended in order to be completed and embodied by the imagination of the observer/occupant. This is why the restrained architectural works of Renzo Piano and Glenn Murcutt achieve greatness: these buildings are clearly and convincingly understandable as conceptual, functional and tectonic structures, yet they avoid overstatement and verbosity, and gently invite our embodied, tactile and sensuous imagination. They are highly rational tectonic structures that project poetic images of gravity and horizon, artifice and nature, use and space, tradition and innovation, materiality and light.

Ontological difference

Art originates in the emergence of the human consciousness of self, and its encounter with the world. Even the oldest of artistic expressions guide us to this simultaneous separation and re-fusion of experience. 'How could the painter or a poet express anything other than his encounter with the world?,' Merleau-Ponty asks.[6] This observation seems to apply to the Stone Age painter as well as to the contemporary artist. The philosopher's remark also applies to the art of architecture as even buildings essentially elaborate this fundamental existential encounter. As a consequence of this mental task, the basic motif of art today is the very same as it was 30,000 years ago. This timeless motif is the enigma of existence.

Architecture is usually understood to originate in the act of dwelling and inhabiting. In my view, however, architecture has a dual origin; it arises simultaneously from the acts of inhabitation and glorification. 'Architecture immortalizes and glorifies something. Hence there can be no architecture where there is nothing to glorify,' Ludwig Wittgenstein argues.[7] Since its very beginning, architecture has structured limitless physical space into distinct places and given space its human measure and meaning. In addition to inhabiting and protecting us in meaningless and hostile physical space, architecture has given us our domicile in cosmic and mental space. 'A house is an instrument with which to confront cosmos,' as Gaston Bachelard suggests.[8]

SENSUOUSLY TECTONIC ARCHITECTURE

To evoke a poetic ambience, architecture does not need to seek spectacular or fantastic imagery. The natural language of architecture arises from the ways it is constructed and assembled. Architectural structures are extensions of nature and they are expected to provide a calming sense of causality and predictability. The art of architecture poeticises construction by turning inevitability into a metaphoric expression. 'Is there anything more mysterious than clarity?' as Paul Valéry asks in his dialogue 'Eupalinos, or the Architect'.

Renzo Piano, The Beyeler Foundation Museum, Basel, Switzerland, 1997.

Piano's museum spaces create optimum conditions for viewing art, without making the building a foreground figure. A great museum enhances works of art instead of presenting itself as a singular work.

Glenn Murcutt, Marika-Alderton House, Yirrkala Community, Eastern Arnheim Land, Northern Territory, Australia, 1991–4. House for an Aboriginal client.

Murcutt's design is a fusion of Australian vernacular ambience and highly rational contemporary construction. The house mediates between past, present and future, and it projects a sense of optimism and courtesy.

Architectural space is not only viewed and observed: it is entered, confronted, encountered, occupied and utilised for specific purposes. The fact that usefulness is a constitutive condition of architecture does not, however, imply that its mental and expressive essence would arise directly from functional and technical preconditions or qualities. The mistake of modern Rationalist thinking from JN Durand to today's routine High-Tech architecture is the belief that technological reason can transcend architectural meanings. Inevitably, the metaphysical and existential dimensions of architecture have their own ontologies and origins. Architecture articulates, metamorphoses and aestheticises the multitude of its rational, physical, technical, utilitarian, social and economic parameters, but its artistic content lies in the distance and tension between these rational qualities and the autonomous architectural imagery, rather than in their reductive fusion.

The opposite reductivism is exemplified by the position of Richard Serra, one of the greatest sculptors of all time. He aggressively opposes the aspiration to fuse architecture and art: 'I would hope that architects could accept the fact that they are architects and are useful as architects, and could stop flirting with the notion of being both artists and architects […] I would think that architects […] would come to understand that they are basically in a service profession, not an artistic endeavour.'[9]

ARCHITECTURE AS SCULPTURE – SCULPTURE AS ARCHITECTURE

During the past few decades, there has been a tendency to regard architecture as sculpture at a grand scale. At the same time, the art of sculpture has moved to architectural scales and contexts. The two spatial and material art forms can surely inspire and illuminate each other, but they have fundamentally different groundings in human experience. Architecture always implies human habitation, and this gives the art of building an ontologically different connection with human mental life.

Tadao Ando, Kidosaki House, Setagaya-ku, Tokyo, 1982–6.

Richard Serra, installation view of the exhibition Richard Serra Sculpture: Forty Years, Museum of Modern Art, New York, 3 June 2007.

Tadao Ando points out the necessary distance and tension between utility and the world of poetic ideas in the art of architecture: 'After having secured the functional basis of a building, I search how far it can be detached from function. Architecture lies in the distance between it and function,' he writes.[10] Due to this internal conceptual distance or split, architecture can also be an artistic expression, contrary to Serra's argument. Indeed, in their condensed abstraction, Ando's works approach the realm of Minimalist art, such as the sculptures of Richard Serra, or the ephemeral light works of James Turrell; in fact, Ando has collaborated with both artists.

Architecture, like all art, aspires to express the human condition, the experience of how we exist in this world. This is the tautological content of works of art regardless of their age and genre. Consequently, the artistic objective of architecture is outside the art form itself in the human existential experience and understanding. Meaningful architecture strengthens our awareness of reality, or rather the enigma of reality, and of the human condition. A touching experience of architecture is always an experience of wonder. In relation to this view, the aspiration to regard architecture as a journey of formal fantasy, or the creation of fictitious architectural narratives, seems misguided.

Poet Randall Jarrell points out the strategy of distancing in the art of painting claimed above in architecture by Ando:

> Solemn things are painted gaily: overwhelmingly expressive things – the Flagellation, for instance – painted inexpressively; [Ambroise] Vollard is painted like an apple, and an apple like the Fall; the female is made male or sexless (as in Michelangelo's *Night*), and a dreaming, acquiescent femininity is made to transfigure a body factually masculine (as in so many of the nude youths on the ceiling of the Sistine Chapel). Between the object and its representation, there is an immense distance: within this distance much of painting lives.[11]

The distance between the realities of making the work and experiencing it is exemplified by the unexpected conflict between Caravaggio's models and his depicted subjects. He is known to have used destitute beggars of his hometown as models for St Joseph and other figures in his paintings, and in his time it was even rumoured that his model for Our Lady was a drowned prostitute whose corpse had been lifted from the River Tiber.[12]

I wish to argue similarly that there is an immense distance between the factual, physical, technical and functional ingredients of an architectural work and their artistic representation, and that the art form of architecture dwells within this gap or distance. These phenomena take place in two separate worlds: the material and technical realities take place in the world of physical and human realities, whereas the poetic 'realities' emerge in an imaginary and mental realm. Indeed, the architect should not be naive or sentimental about the usefulness or rationality of his work, and buildings should not be taken at their face value any more than any other works of art. Besides, architectural expression, as any artistic expression, always has yet another double focus; it takes place within the internal discourse and history of the discipline itself, while it is also an autonomous individual and existential expression. Architecture is about architecture and the existential and lived world, at the same time.

Architecture frames, structures, re-orients, scales, refocuses and slows down our experience of the world and makes it an ingredient of the embodied sense of our own being; it always has a mediating role instead of being the end itself. Regardless of their inherent characteristics as abstracted architecture, the room-size sculptures of Serra, the light spaces of James Turrell and the spatial structures of Robert Irwin belong inevitably and irreversibly to the realm of artistic imagery, whereas Luis Barragán's often similarly abstracted and painterly spaces are equally convincingly profound architecture. This view should not be taken as an argument of difference in quality, only of the fundamental difference in the ontological origin and intentionality of different art forms.

Significance of origins

In his book *ABC of Reading*, Ezra Pound emphasises the significance of origins in the arts: '… [M]usic begins to atrophy when it departs too far from dance […] poetry begins to atrophy when it gets too far from music …'.[13] Similarly, in my view, architecture turns into mere visual aesthetics when it departs from its originary motives of domesticating space and time for human occupation and the metaphoric representation of the act of construction. This is the point where today's computerised and formalistic virtuosity seems to fall off the track of architecture. Architecture cannot be a pure and autonomously artistic fabrication of space and form as its very purpose is to structure, articulate and express real human existence and life. Through time, architecture has been rooted in lived reality in different ways. In the periods of prevailing vernacular or stylistic conventions, this process of rooting took place on an unconscious and collective level, whereas in modernity, the fundamental motifs are more individual, and perhaps also more conscious. The meaning of architecture arises unconsciously from below, from its use and existential task, and it cannot be projected through a purely conceptual or methodical operation by the designer, or the computer, for that matter. The art of architecture is not a matter of invention but of interpretation; it does, of course, contain technological and syntactic innovations and novelties, but its mental essence cannot be an invention as it is rooted in the realities of life. When the enigma of existence is lost, architecture turns into meaningless fabrication and construction, at best a demonstration of technical and retinal virtuosity.

When expressing a critical view of today's architecture, one needs to specify whether one is speaking of the normal, and often relatively anonymous construction in various countries, or the formalist architecture that draws the attention of the international media. The first category is often down-to-earth and tied to a tradition, but does not produce spectacular and novel enough images to be celebrated by the media.

Every art form needs to be reconnected with its originary essence. This requirement is of particular significance in periods when the art form in question tends to turn into an empty aestheticised mannerism. This argument is not an expression of architectural conservatism, but of common sense, and a respectful acknowledgement of the continuum of human culture and life. As TS Eliot argues: 'No poet, no artist of any art, has his complete meaning alone. His significance, his appreciation is the appreciation of his relation to the dead poets and artists. You cannot value him alone; you must set him, for contrast

ARCHITECTURE AND ART

Since their origins, architecture and art have interacted with each other. Also, the development of modern architecture ran parallel to the emergence of modern art. During the decades of the prevailing International Style, art was most often regarded merely as enriching and beautifying objects in an architectural context. An equally misguided attitude is to reject the crucial difference of the art forms. Luis Barragán's architectural spaces approach imaginary painterly spaces, yet they are always spaces of human occupation and activity, instead of spaces of mere aesthetic contemplation.

Luis Barragán, Francisco Gilardi House, Mexico City, 1975–7. Collaborator: Alberto Chauvet.

This architectural space is a corner of the dining room of the house; reflections, light and colour turn the space into a weightless painterly abstraction.

Robert Irwin, 1234, 1992. Three voile tergal (scrim) walls, violet, green, black acrylic lacquer. Front to back 4.27 m × 11.58 m, each, three walls 3.05 m × 7.92 m, each, five frames.

Due to their scale and inherent spatiality, Irwin's works usually project strong architectural connotations.

and comparison, among the dead.'[14] The final assessor of an artistic work is the continued process of tradition, not contemporaries, or even less, the author him/herself.

Louis Kahn's great contribution was his rediscovery of the ontological essence of various aspects of architecture; what the building wants to be and what the ageless traditions of this art form are, instead of what the momentary author, not to speak of what the computer, might want. His work exudes an archaic emotive power in comparison with the contemporaneous architecture of the International Style that is merely a product of rationality, technique and a reductive aestheticised stylistic canon.

Kahn preached the importance of beginnings:

> The spirit of the start is the most marvellous moment at any time for anything. Because in the start lies the seed for all things that must follow. A thing is unable to start unless it can contain all that ever can come from it. That is the characteristic of a beginning, otherwise it is no beginning – it is a false beginning.[15]

Kahn's architecture projects pregnant imageries that open up new potentials for expression regardless of his use of eternal geometry, and the stylistically often unpolished character of his works. Paradoxically, he gave architecture new beginnings by returning back to its very origins in Egypt, Greece and Rome.

Architectural works that echo the tremors of origins – such as the works of Sigurd Lewerentz, Luis Barragán, Louis Kahn, Aldo van Eyck, Sverre Fehn, Alvaro Siza and Peter Zumthor, for example, project an authoritative presence and depth of feeling. Such works are not necessarily always aesthetically refined or elegant, as they pose a deep and disturbing emotive power.

Today, Steven Holl's buildings deliberately accommodate conflicts, disturbances and tensions in order to give a breath of life to the excessively stylised architecture of our time. He aspires to look at architecture at its point of origin, as a potential, not as something given, or an aesthetic and formal prejudice. Holl's recently completed Knut Hamsun Centre in Hamarøy (1999–2010), beyond the Polar Circle in northern Norway, exemplifies an approach to architecture that arises from its site and specific characteristics of the task, not a preconceived architectural language (illustration, opposite, left). The twisted,

THE NOVEL ARCHITECTURAL IMAGE

A profound, unforeseen architectural image is not a formal invention as it grows from the unique characteristic of the context, and task, as well as the author's deep delving into the essence of architecture. A novel architecture is more an excavation and exploration than an invention. Architectural language does not arise from mere formal invention but rather from below, from grasping the human essence of architecture anew. True architectural insight always spans the ancient and the novel, the primordial and the refined.

Steven Holl, Knut Hamsun Center, Hamarøy, Norway (1999–2010).

The building incorporates episodes of the writer's works in its architectural language, and turns into a built portrait of its subject.

Peter Zumthor, Bruder Klaus Chapel, Mechernich, Germany, 2007. Model of lead floor and water.

The interior gives the impression of a mythological cave that is a battleground between darkness and light. The cast concrete surface mirrors its wooden formwork that has been burned away.

black-tarred tower arises above its fabulous natural landscape and ordinary Norwegian village scene as an enigmatic figure that invites identification and interpretation. The Centre turns into an architectural portrait of the controversial Norwegian literary giant who shattered his own cultural esteem in his later years with his Nazi sympathies. Holl's architecture also adapts scenes of the writer's literary works as episodes in the architectural ensemble. At the same time, the building is a camera obscura for viewing the extraordinary landscape and focusing on distinct aspects of the setting that also figure in Hamsun's literary works.

The lived metaphor

I have suggested above that both artistic and architectural images are metaphoric representations of the world and the human condition. Artistic images are external to us, whereas architectural images are integrated with our very life and sense of self; we exist and understand our existence through architecture, or the man-made world at large. Again, this is not an argument of a difference in quality, but in essence. The irrefutable and constant presence of architecture is simultaneously its weakness and strength. It is a weakness in the sense that we tend to become blind to the characteristics and qualities of our settings and buildings, and instead of being independent artistic foreground statements they usually have their silent but permanent impact as frames of our unconscious pre-understanding. As a consequence, we tend to become conscious of architecture only when it fails, not when it performs its task in an expected manner.

Bachelard criticises the Heideggerian idea of the primal human anxiety resulting from being thrown into the world, on the grounds that instead of being cast into an unstructured and meaningless world, we are always born into an architecturally prestructured world. 'The house is a large cradle,' Bachelard argues implying that as humans, we are born in this cradle of architecture.[16] An artistic work, such as a painting or a poem, can be emotionally powerful and moving, and it can redirect our entire personality, but it does not form a silent cradle for our everyday existence and activities in the way that architecture does.

Louis Kahn gives architecture an encompassing task: 'The realm of architecture is a realm within which all other things are. In the realm of architecture there is sculpture, there is painting, there is physics, there is music – everything is in it.'[17] I do not suggest that architecture is 'the mother of arts', as has been claimed, I simply wish to re-emphasise the fundamental ontological difference between architecture and works of art, and the specific mental constitution of architecture, as well as its uniquely grounded impact on human life and culture.

A profound architectural experience can have a transformative impact. As I visited the Curutchet House (1949) in Argentina designed by Le Corbusier, the forceful spatiality of the building recalibrated my entire sense of orientation: below and above, left and right, near and far (illustration, opposite, left). Even back in Finland, on the other side of the globe, I felt that I was experiencing the world through this extraordinary architectural instrument at the edge of a park in the city of La Plata, now internalised as sensory and embodied memories in my body. This personal experience underscores the unexpected corporeal and mental impact of an architectural metaphor.

Both artistic and architectural works are existential metaphors in which an entire world is reflected. Iconic buildings, such as Casa Malaparte (1938–40) on Capri, the Melnikov House (1927–9) in Moscow, Pierre Chareau's Maison de Verre (1929) in Paris, are condensed metaphoric microcosms, inhabited and lived metaphors, self-sufficient universes enclosed within the walls of these structures.

ARCHITECTURAL METAPHORS AND ICONS

Profound examples of architecture are condensed metaphors of the world and human existence. They guide and condition perceptions and experiences, and structure human thought even as absent but memorised images.

Iconic buildings are unique and exhaustive representatives of a certain genre or type. An iconic building exudes a sense of authority, perfection and finality; it simultaneously opens up and closes a vision.

Le Corbusier, The Curutchet House, La Plata, Argentina, 1948–9.

The house is a forcefully spatial architectural configuration which is experienced in an exceptionally embodied manner.

Konstantin Melnikov, The Melnikov House, Moscow, Russia, 1927–9. Axonometric drawing.

The house is an architectural icon that exudes mysterious signification and enigma.

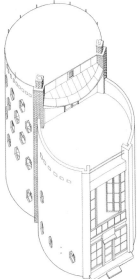

Both Casa Malaparte and the Melnikov House exude a metaphysical air. The Casa Malaparte occupies its position authoritatively on a nearly vertical rock formation on the island of Capri, giving both the rocky site and the open horizon of the Mediterranean a heightened experiential and metaphysical meaning. The roof terrace, devoid of any protective handrails, turns into an abstracted plateau, a weightless place, a stage and a sacrificial altar, suspended between heaven and earth. The tapered stairway leading to the roof terrace points at the sky like Jacob's ladder.

The Melnikov House, composed of two intersecting cylinders (circles in the plan form), has the image of the juxtaposed halos of two saints in a Russian icon painting (illustration, above, right). The fenestration of vertically elongated hexagonal windows turns the house into an astronomical instrument, and a spectacular device of ritualised illumination. In the middle of the historical layers of central Moscow, and the commonality of Soviet and Russian life, this house appears as an alien object, a spaceship from an unknown planet. This cosmic and awe-inspiring aura must have safeguarded the house as the private residence of the architect's family through the decades of Communist rule, when private property was otherwise turned into collective ownership.

The Maison de Verre is a radically modern house and dense metaphor for culture, industrial production and metropolitan life. It is a meticulously conceived technological and functional device that exudes a mechanistic but poeticised air. It is a fetish of technology, and a tour-de-force of mechanisation and mobile architectural elements, a house as an obsessive device and a 'Bachelor Machine'. The house exemplifies the capacity and desire of profound architecture to transcend its utilitarian and technical prerequisites and turn into a metaphoric representation of the metaphysical realm, the realm beyond everyday concerns and consciousness.

Thinking through art

Ideas articulated by the arts are painterly, sculptural, musical, theatrical, cinematic and architectural embodied propositions, conceived and expressed through the inherent medium and artistic logic of the particular art form in a dialectical process with its own history and traditions. Artistic ideas arise from an existential understanding and desire, and they are not ideational or translatable into verbal interpretations or explanations. They are embodied existential metaphors.

All significant architecture is a result of serious thinking, or rather, of a distinct way of thinking through the medium of architecture. In the same way that film is a mode of cinematic thought and painting a means of articulating painterly ideas, architecture implies philosophising through the specific material means of constructing, as distilled and grasped through the acts of dwelling and occupation. The mother tongue of architecture arises from its tectonic materiality, and the way that the physical structure takes its particular shape and details under the causalities of gravity, climate, construction and use. These are important considerations also for architectural education, as its primary task must be to promote genuine architectural thinking, rather than general intellectual rationalisation or aestheticisation, or a mere application of stylistic preferences.

Art and architecture do not demonstrate or mimic ideas of philosophy; they are modes of embodied and existential thinking in their own right. According to Constantin Brancusi: 'Art generates ideas, it doesn't represent them – which means that a true work of art comes into being intuitively, without preconceived motives, because it *is* the motive and there can be no accounting for it a priori.'[18]

In my own collaborations with painters, sculptors and craftsmen, over five decades, I have learned immensely from their capacity to think through their eyes, hands, skin and body. Artists and craftsmen think through the existential knowledge accumulated in the silent wisdom of the body and the traditions of the art form/craft itself. Architecture is philosophically a complex, conflicting and 'impure' discipline, and as a consequence, it calls for an approach that combines research and innovation, trial and error, thinking and intuition, rationality and emotion, cognition and embodiment, identification and projection, sight and foresight.

Several recent provocative philosophical studies on the embodied nature of thinking oblige us to reconsider the body–mind divide and the essence of intelligence and thinking itself.[19] Architecture and art operate within this gap between a pre-reflective and embodied wisdom, existential knowledge and cerebral understanding.

The American philosopher Richard Rorty makes the ultimate statement on the significance of the body for the very essence of human existence: 'If the body had been easier to understand, nobody would have thought that we had a mind.'[20] In addition to embodiment, the physical act of making is an inseparable part of the creative process. Joseph Brodsky, the poet, discusses the role of craft in poetry as follows:

> No honest craftsman or maker knows in the process of working whether he is making or creating. [...] The first, the second, and the last reality for him is the work itself, the very process of working. The process takes precedence over its result, if only because the latter is impossible without the former [...] In reality (in art and, I would think, science), experience and the accompanying expertise are the maker's worst enemies.[21]

It seems to me that here the poet somewhat exaggerates the significance of the process, as the result, the final work, must also be a crucial motive and intention. Yet Georges Braque, also, valued the inception of painting: 'With me, the inception of a work always takes precedence over the results anticipated.'[22]

This is yet another essential perspective for artistic and architectural education; instead of being intellectual preconceptions or fabrications, artistic images arise from, and are articulated through, the maker's sense of self and the very act of making.

Historicity of the mind and poetic time

Art, and architecture, are often – and particularly today – seen solely as a search for the novel and the unforeseen. This biased emphasis on novelty has distorted the understanding of the essence of the artistic endeavour. Referring to Friedrich Hölderlin's idea of the romantic logic of transgression that always searches for something new in order to avoid being bored with the old, the Norwegian philosopher Lars Svendsen argues that: 'as the new is searched only due to its newness, everything becomes identical, because it has no other properties but its newness'.[23] Yet art is, in my view, fundamentally engaged in the opposite aspiration; it seeks to re-animate, re-mythologise, re-enchant, re-sensualise and re-eroticise our relation with the world, and momentarily lure back the originary mode of undifferentiated and oceanic consciousness of our early infancy. This mental 'regression' of awareness is equally essential in architecture. Art seeks a lost world rather than an unconquered territory, or perhaps we should rather think that the two objectives are united as the image of the primordial and mythical Ouroboros snake that swallows its own tail.

However, in revitalising what already exists in our mental worlds, art has to use means of mental and poetic magic. Recent neurological research promises to deepen our understanding of the origins of aesthetic pleasure and the evolutionary significance of beauty. 'I recognize that the unconscious mind can be nothing other than a neurological process, but that meaning is in some unknown fashion potentially present as a latent property,' Arnold H Modell suggests.[24] He uses the intriguing notion 'the biology of meaning', while stating that 'a crucial problem for neuroscience is to explain how matter becomes imagination'.[25] I have earlier suggested that our certain perceptual and neural patterns and behaviours are likely to be biologically motivated.

In my view, it is beyond doubt that our existentially most significant perceptions, reactions and emotions are bound to be associated with our biological evolutionary course as a species of the living world. To see aesthetic pleasure or metaphysical concerns as an anti-evolutionary development, as mere momentary sensory inventions and fashions, does not seem plausible. Awareness and consciousness in the animal world are inadequately understood, but there is evidence that the pleasure principle, that has been identified even in the most primitive worms, has gradually developed into systems of choice based on visual, or 'aesthetic' difference, as in the case of mate selection or the display nests of bowerbirds.

Architecture is commonly understood as the art form of space, but it is equally significantly a means of articulating time. At the same time that it domesticates meaningless natural and 'wild' space, it gives endless physical time a human measure and turns it into cultured and human time. Art and architecture help us to confront the 'terror of time', to use the thought-provoking notion of Karsten Harries.

Poetry confronts us with images at the very emergence of language, painting makes us see objects and things as if they had not been glimpsed by the human eye before, and architecture re-confronts us with gravity, the elements, the realities of life, and the wonder of construction, as if space were claimed for human occupation for the first time. The novelty and freshness of the timeless is the true miracle of the artistic image.

At the same time that great works of art make us aware of time and the layering of culture, they halt time in images that are eternally new. This is already the magic of the most ancient images of rock art in Africa and Australia. Regardless of the fact that these images may have been painted nearly 50,000 years ago, the animals depicted in these paintings are being hunted right in front of our eyes, and we can sense the determined focus of the hunters and the panicked attempt of the animals to escape. We can even hear the excited racket of the hunt.

Usually we understand artistic images as an emotional manipulation of form, but art is equally significantly a manipulation of the temporal and evolutionary layers of the mind. Art fuses the child with the adult, and the originary savage with the processes of enculturation. In that essential sense, art is at the service of evolutionary understanding and recollection of our past. Significantly, it defends and protects our mental past and extends its capacities. 'Art [is] an extension of the functions of the visual brain in its search for essentials,' as Semir Zeki, the neurologist argues.[26]

Unity of the arts: art and life

'One of the characteristic symptoms of the spiritual condition of our age', observed Baudelaire when writing about Delacroix, is that, 'the arts aspire, if not to take one another's place, at least reciprocally to lend one another new powers.'[27] It seems as if Baudelaire were here describing the artistic scene of the end of the second millennium rather than of his own time in the mid-1800s. Rosalind Krauss's essay 'Sculpture in the Expanded Field' (1978) comes immediately to mind as an example of the kind of fusion suggested by Baudelaire. Krauss analyses the crossing of boundaries between landscape, architecture and sculpture, characteristic of the late 20th century.[28] She concludes that contemporary sculpture can only be defined in an exclusive manner, that is, through what *it is not*. She defines sculpture through the categories of *not-landscape* and *not-architecture*, and she introduces three new realms of sculpture: *site-construction*, *marked sites* and *axiomatic structures* to expand the traditional notion of sculpture as an object. Similar new hybrid realms have emerged in other art forms as well.

In addition to the fact that various art forms are expanding their respective fields and being cross-fertilised, arts have a common mental and experiential ground: the human condition. Alvar Aalto, for one, writes about this 'common root' of the arts:

> Abstract art forms have brought impulses to the architecture of our time, although indirectly, but this fact cannot be denied. On the other hand, architecture has provided sources for abstract art. These two art forms have alternatively influenced each other. There we are – the arts do have a common root even in our time [...][29]

In another context, Aalto emphasises the intuitive and emotional ground of art:

> Abstract art at its best is the result of a kind of crystallization process. Perhaps that is why it can be grasped only intuitively. Though in and behind the work of art there are constructive thoughts and elements of human tragedy. In a way it is a medium that can transport us directly into the human current of feelings that has almost been lost by written word.[30]

Aalto's use of the concept 'abstract' can be understood in relation to the Modernist ideological view of his time, but he could just as well have made the same arguments of art in general.

It is evident that the architect can be inspired by other art forms and we can benefit from studying aspects of our own craft in other artistic disciplines. Literary, painterly and cinematic. For example, imageries can inspire architectural thought or be directly applied in architectural contexts. In fact, as architects, we can today identify what has been lost in our art form through studying other arts that have not been instrumentalised and conventionalised to the same degree as the art of architecture. I have personally found it very invigorating and inspiring to encounter other art forms from painting and sculpture, music and dance, poetry and theatre, to today's installation, video and land art. I have also found it rewarding to teach architecture through the architectural imageries in other art forms and their utilisation of space. As the art of architecture tends to be dominated by rationality, it is particularly instructive to reveal the importance of the emotional dimension of poetic imagery through other art forms.

The essential connections and parallels between architecture, painting and sculpture during the Modernist period are well known. Also today the cross pollination between architecture, earth art and Minimalist art is evident. However, even structures, rhythms and images of music have been applied in architecture as in the collaborations of Iannis Xenakis with Le Corbusier as well as in the independent work of this architect/composer. The Pythagorean harmonic tradition represents a nearly two and a half millennia long exploration into the harmonic commonalities of music and architecture, hearing and vision.[31] The Pythagorean tradition was revived in the Renaissance and, again, in the 20th century by Hans Kayser at the Vienna Academy of Music as well as in the harmonic and proportional studies of two architects, RM Schindler (1887–1953) in the United States and Aulis Blomstedt (1906–79) in Finland. Blomstedt developed a system of harmonic measures and proportions which he called *Canon 60*, based on the arithmetic factors of number 60 and musical intervals (illustration, page 112, left).

Along with scientific and conceptual metaphors and images, Steven Holl has used musical metaphors and analogues in his architectural work. The Stretto House in Dallas, Texas (1989–91) is based on the musical concept of *stretto* (a fugue motif used to accompany itself to form a counterpoint) and Béla Bartók's *Music for Strings, Percussion and Celeste* (illustration, page 112, right). The four movements of the musical score, as well as its subdivision into percussion (heavy) and string (light) components, are reflected in the spatial, formal and material structures of the house. Another example of a musical inspiration in Holl's work is the project for the Sarphatistraat Offices in

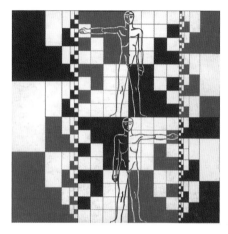
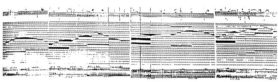

Amsterdam (1996–2000); the reflected light and colour, trapped behind the perforated metal facades, echo a concept deriving from the music of Morton Feldman's *Patterns in a Chromatic Field*.[32]

'To a large extent', says poet Wallace Stevens, 'the problems of poets are problems of painters, and poets must often turn to the literature or painting for a discussion of their own problems.'[33] In another context he writes: 'I suppose … that it would be possible to study poetry by studying painting.'[34] It is, indeed, noteworthy that numerous poets have written significant essays on artists, particularly painters: Wallace Stevens, Rainer Maria Rilke, DH Lawrence and William Carlos Williams on Paul Cézanne alone. Rilke has also written knowledgeably and touchingly about the art of Auguste Rodin,[35] after all, as a young man he served as the master sculptor's secretary in Paris for a considerable time (1902–06). On the other hand, buildings and architectural metaphors appear frequently in poetry and novels. Yet, I do not know of significant writings by poets on architects or architecture in our time. Perhaps, this observation reveals something about our art form, poets may not any more regard architecture as an art form or inspiring enough for verse. However, occasional architectural images and metaphors figure frequently in poetry, as in the poems and imaginative prose of my countryman Bo Carpelan (1926–).[36]

In my personal case, painting, sculpture and cinema, along with poetry and novels, have been important for my understanding of the essence of my own craft. Paintings, films and literary works have revealed to me the essential connections of life, space, buildings, cities and the human mind. These lessons

ARCHITECTURE AND MUSIC

The two art forms have been connected particularly through shared theories of harmonic proportion. Renaissance theories revived the Pythagorean ideas of world harmony. The Pythagorean tradition was again reintroduced in the 20th century by Hans Kayser in Vienna and Aulis Blomstedt in Helsinki. In some cases, such as Steven Holl's Stretto House, musical structures have been directly applied in architectural composition.

Aulis Blomstedt, study of Pythagorean intervals applied to the human measure of 180 cm, early 1960s.

Steven Holl, Stretto House, Dallas, Texas, 1989–91. Parts of Béla Bartók's score for the four movements of Music for Strings, Percussion, and Celeste, and a model view of Steven Holl's project for the Stretto House.

have taught me not to regard my discipline merely as a visual formalism, convention or rhetoric.

Today the blurring of the boundaries between architecture and sculpture as well as architecture and cinema, theatre, dance and performance art is evident. The works of installation and performance artists, such as Ann Hamilton, Marina Abramović and Rebecca Horn, and video artists like Bill Viola, often have architectural connotations. In addition to the disappearance of boundaries, other art forms articulate and express architectural images and situations; I have myself written a book on architectural imagery in cinema viewed through the notion of existential space, a concept that provides a shared experiential ground for these two art forms.[37] Cinema teaches us how the poetic dimension can be fully integrated with a sense of life.

Aestheticisation and beauty

Among artists themselves, aesthetics is usually regarded as a shallow and formalist approach to artistic phenomena. Barnett Newman's exclamation, 'Aesthetics is for artists what ornithology is for birds,' exemplifies this deprecating attitude.[38] The notion of aesthetics carries, of course, a density of meanings and practices. On a general level, I am interested in the aesthetic intention as an inherent yearning for beauty and a better world, and as a biological principle, rather than as a formal analysis of artistic products and intention.

Through the entire modern era, the notion of beauty has been a rather suspect notion. In recent literary and philosophical writings, however, such as Elaine Scarry's *On Beauty and Being Just* and Martha Nussbaum's *Poetic Justice*, beauty and aesthetics are reconnected with the ethical dimension.[39] Recent neurological studies, such as Semir Zeki's *Inner Vision: An Exploration of Art and the Brain* (1999), John Onians' *Neuroarthistory: From Aristotle and Pliny to Baxandall and Zeki* (2007), Arnold H Modell's *Imagination and the Meaningful Brain* (2006) and Harry Francis Mallgrave's *The Architect's Brain: Neuroscience, Creativity, and Architecture* (2010), connect interestingly aesthetic phenomena with our mental and neurological constitution.

Joseph Brodsky firmly believed in the significance of the aesthetic sense, and even argued that our ethical sense is born of aesthetic judgement. 'Aesthetics is the Mother of ethics,'[40] and 'Human being is an aesthetic creature before he is an ethical one,'[41] the poet believes. He goes even further in his view of the foundational role of beauty. 'The purpose of evolution, believe it or not, is beauty,' he states with the assurance of a master poet.[42]

In my view, idealism, optimism, justice and hope are all connected with the desire and passion for beauty. Beauty and the power of imagination also co-exist, as the experience of beauty necessarily arises from the fusion of perception and desire, reality and idealisation, observation and compassion. A civilisation has hope only as long as it can distinguish between beauty and ugliness, between what is genuinely desirable and what should be avoided. When a civilisation loses its sense and desire for beauty, it also loses its sense of what is just, and it is doomed to decline.

Aestheticisation and ritualisation are means of projecting significance on to cultural events and phenomena, but they are equally powerful means of concealing less benevolent and hidden intentions; aestheticisation is often a means of hiding and covering up. From its originary role of liberation and protection, architecture also can turn into a vehicle of oppression. Herbert Read makes a rather shocking remark of this dual face of aestheticisation: 'Classicism […] represents for us now, and has always represented, the forces of oppression. Classicism is the intellectual counterpart of political tyranny […] whenever the blood of martyrs stains the ground, there you will find a Doric column or perhaps a statue of Minerva.'[43] In the same manner, images of transparency in today's buildings frequently mask hierarchical power structures, dictatorial schemes and exploitative economic strategies.

Cynical intentions can be concealed in apparent order and forced sentimental beauty. There is a fundamental difference between beauty as a genuine and autonomous individual experience and as a social convention of overt style and aestheticisation. Paul Valéry's notion of the 'tyranny of beauty' applies to the use of a distinct aesthetic language for purposes of suppression.[44] The manipulative beauty is usually thematised and shallowly and naively symbolic; the innate multi-dimensionality and independence of art is harnessed to the service of a deliberate mental manipulation. Throughout history, architecture has glorified power and domination by means of its commanding language of order and authority. Today's thematised and aestheticised architectural images often mask shameless economic, ideological and cultural exploitation.

In addition to being the Age of the Image, our time is also the Age of Aestheticisation; all kinds of merchandise, politics, operations, and even war, are aestheticised and turned into shallow entertainment. Also, art and architecture tend to be aestheticised and detached from their existential and autonomous ground. 'Novel' art works are produced deliberately for an art market that indiscriminately values novelty as the highest artistic quality. Art has turned from being an authentic existential expression into a forceful invention and fabrication of marketable newness. As a consequence of this development, the arts are in danger of losing their existential sincerity and turning into mere speculative aesthetics, a glossy and seductive, but empty and alienating surface. Joseph Brodsky even criticises his esteemed colleague, Ezra Pound, for aestheticisation: 'His mistake is an old one; aiming at beauty [...] beauty cannot be targeted, it is a result of other, and often very ordinary pursuits.'[45]

Through their origination in authentic individual experience, profound works of art and architecture always defend the autonomy and emancipation of individual experience, and they form a counterforce to calculation and exploitation. Art safeguards the foundations of individual mental autonomy and dignity. This, in my view, is the shared and most invaluable task of all arts. In a world which is in danger of collapsing into uniformity and meaninglessness – regardless of its explicit claim for the diversification of experience – the human task of the arts has a heightened significance.

In accordance with Rilke's view of the demanding mental preconditions for the emergence of a profound line of verse, I wish to suggest that architecture does not merely arise from rationalisations of the building task, mere aesthetic aspirations or the desire for recognition and fame. Architecture also arises from the deepest of existential encounters and concerns. The task of architecture is not to beautify life, but to reinforce and reveal its existential essence, beauty and enigma.

References

1 Elaine Scarry, *Dreaming by the Book*, Princeton University Press (Princeton, NJ), 1999, p 7.

2 Gaston Bachelard, *Water and Dreams: An Essay On the Imagination of Matter*, Pegasus Foundation (Dallas, TX), 1999, p 16.

3 *Borges on Writing*, edited by Norman Thomas di Giovanni, Daniel Halpern and Frank MacShane, Ecco Press (Hopewell, NJ), 1994, p 45.

4 Ibid. p 48.

5 As quoted in Peter von Bagh, 'The Death of Emotion', *Synnyt: Sources of Contemporary Art*, Museum of Contemporary Art (Helsinki), 1989, p 202.

6 As quoted in Richard Kearney, *Modern Movements in European Philosophy* (Manchester and New York), 1994, p 82.

7 *Ludwig Wittgenstein, Culture and Value*, Georg Henrik von Wright in collaboration with Heikki Nyman, editors, Blackwell (Oxford), 1998, p 74e.

8 Gaston Bachelard, *Poetics of Space*, Beacon Press (Boston), 1969, p 46.

9 Richard Serra, 'An Optional Museum Goer – Interview with Brendan Richardson', in *Richard Serra, Writings/Interviews*, University of Chicago Press (Chicago and London), 1994, p 109.

10 Tadao Ando, 'The Emotionally Made Architectural Spaces of Tadao Ando', in *The Japan Architect* (April 1980), 45–6.

11 Randall Jarrell, 'Against Abstract Expressionism', JD McClatchy, editor, *Poets on Painters*, University of California Press (Berkeley), 1990, pp 187–8.

12 Richard Kearney, *The Wake of Imagination*, Routledge (London), 1994, pp 136–7.

13 Ezra Pound, *ABC of Reading*, New Directions (New York), 1987, p 14.

14 TS Eliot, 'Tradition and the Individual Talent', *Selected Essays*, new edition, Harcourt, Brace & World (New York), 1964.

15 Louis I Kahn, 'New Frontiers in Architecture: CIAM in Otterlo, 1959', in Alessandra Latour, editor, *Louis I Kahn: Writings, Lectures, Interviews*, Rizzoli International Publications (New York), 1991, p 85.

16 Bachelard, *Poetics of Space*, 1969, p 7.

17 Kahn, *Louis I Kahn*, 1991, p 93.

18 Constantin Brancusi quoted in M Gale, editor, 'Selected Aphorisms', *Constantin Brancusi: The Essence of Things*, Tate Publishing (London), 2004, p 133.

19 For instance: Mark Johnson, *The Body in the Mind: The Bodily Basis of Meaning, Imagination, and Reason*, University of Chicago Press (Chicago and London), 1987; and George Lakoff and Mark Johnson, *Philosophy in the Flesh: The Embodied Mind and Its Challenge to Western Thought*, Basic Books (New York), 1999.

Harry Francis Mallgrave's recent book *The Architect's Brain: Neuroscience, Creativity and Architecture*, John Wiley & Sons (Chichester, West Sussex), 2010, directly applies views and findings in neuroscience and philosophy to the field of architecture.

20 Richard Rorty, *Philosophy and the Mirror of Nature*, Princeton University Press (Evanston, IL), 1979, p 239.

21 Joseph Brodsky, 'A Cat's Meow', *On Grief and Reason*, Farrar, Straus and Giroux (New York), 1997, p 302.

22 As quoted in Gaston Bachelard, *The Right to Dream*, Dallas Institute Publications (Dallas, TX), 1983, p 51.

23 Lars Fr H Svendsen, *Ikävystymisen filosofia* [*The Philosophy of Boredom*], Kustannusosakeyhtiö Tammi (Helsinki), 2005, p 75. Trans Juhani Pallasmaa.

24 Arnold H Modell, *Imagination and the Meaningful Brain*, MIT Press (Cambridge, MA and London, UK), 2006, p XII.

25 Modell, *Imagination and the Meaningful Brain*, 2006, p 1.

26 Semir Zeki, *Inner Vision: An Exploration of Art and the Brain*, Oxford University Press (Oxford), 1999, p 22.

27 As quoted in McClatchy, *Poets on Painters*, 1990, XII.

28 Rosalind Krauss, 'Sculpture in the Expanded Field', in Hal Foster, editor, *Postmodern Culture*, Pluto Press (London and Sydney), 1985, pp 31–42.

29 Quoted in Kirmo Mikkola, *Aalto*, Gummerus (Jyväskylä), 1985, p 42. The origin of the quotation is unidentified.

30 Alvar Aalto, 'The Trout and the Mountain Stream', in Göran Schildt, editor, trans Stuart Wrede, *Sketches, Alvar Aalto*, MIT Press (Cambridge, MA), 1985, p 85.

31 For the Pythagorean harmonics, see Hans Kayser, *Lehrbuch der Harmonie*, Occident Verlag (Zurich), 1950. For a contemporary application of Pythagorean harmonics, see *Aulis Blomstedt, Architect: Pensée et Forme, Etudes Harmoniques*, Juhani Pallasmaa, editor, Museum of Finnish Architecture (Helsinki), 1977;

and *RM Schindler: Composition and Construction*, edited by Lionel March and Judith Sheine, Academy Editions and Ernst & Sohn (London and Berlin), 1993, pp 88–101.

32 *Stretto House: Steven Holl*, Monacelli Press (New York), 1996.

33 As quoted in Charles Tomlinson, 'The Poet as Painter', in McClatchy, *Poets on Painters*, 1990, p 266.

34 Wallace Stevens, 'The Relations between Poetry and Painting', in McClatchy, *Poets on Painters*, 1990, p 111.

35 Rainer Maria Rilke, *Auguste Rodin*, translated from the German by Daniel Slager, Archipelago Books (New York), 2004.

36 Bo Carpelan (b 1926). For his poetry translated into English see: Bo Carpelan, *Homecoming*, translated from Finland-Swedish by David McDuff, Carcanet (Manchester), 1993; and for his prose: Bo Carpelan, *Urwind*, translated from Finland-Swedish by David McDuff, Northwestern University Press (Evanston, IL), 1993.

37 Juhani Pallasmaa, *The Architecture of Image: Existential Space in Cinema*, Rakennustieto Oy (Helsinki), 2001.

38 Harold Rosenberg, *Barnett Newman*, Harry N Abrams (New York), 1978, p 43.

39 See, Elaine Scarry, *On Beauty and Being Just*, Princeton University Press (New York), 1999; and Martha C Nussbaum, *Poetic Justice: The Literary Imagination and Public Life*, Beacon Press (Boston), 1995.

40 Joseph Brodsky, *On Grief and Reason*, Farrar, Straus and Giroux (New York), 1997, p 36.

41 Ibid. p 50.

42 Ibid. 'An Immodest Proposal', p 207.

43 Herbert Read, *The Philosophy of Modern Art*, Meridian Books (New York), 1965, pp 112–13.

44 'What is most beautiful is of necessity tyrannical ...'. Paul Valéry, 'Eupalinos, or the Architect', *Dialogues*, Pantheon Books (New York), 1956, p 86.

45 Joseph Brodsky, *Watermark*, Penguin Books (London), 1992, p 70.

5
The architectural image

Our house is our corner of the world … it is our first universe, a real cosmos in every sense of the word. … It is an instrument with which to confront the cosmos.[1]

Gaston Bachelard

Buildings are frequently presented detached from their contexts of landscape, culture and social reality. They are also shown and reviewed as independent aesthetic objects separated from the world view, or the image of life, and values which they communicate. Yet, architectural works are bound to be highly condensed metaphoric representations of culture, and these metaphoric images guide and organise our perceptions and thoughts.

Architectural images are related to specific acts and, consequently, buildings are always essentially invitations and verbs. The architectural images that can move our emotions are grounded in our unconscious reactions and biological historicity.

Architecture and the world

In our time, architecture is threatened by two opposite processes: instrumentalisation and aestheticisation. On the one hand, our secular, materialist and quasi-rational culture is turning buildings into mere instrumental structures, devoid of mental meaning, for the purposes of utility and economy. On the other hand, in order to draw attention and facilitate instant seduction, architecture is increasingly turning into the fabrication of seductively aestheticised images without roots in our existential experience and devoid of authentic desire of life. Instead of being a lived and embodied existential metaphor, today's architecture tends to project purely retinal images, architectural pictures as it were, for the seduction of the eye. Yet, the task of architecture is not only to provide physical shelter, facilitate activities and stimulate sensory pleasure. In addition to being externalisations and extensions of human bodily functions, buildings are also mental extensions and projections, they are externalisations of our imagination, memory and conceptual capacities. Towns and buildings, as well as other man-made objects, structure our existential experiences and give them specific meanings. Man-made structures 'tame' the world for human habitation and understanding, but they also enhance its sensuality and desirability. The world outside our house is a different world from the one confronted without the mediating effect of the architectural artefact. A storm raging outside the window or above the roof, is a different storm to the one experienced without the sheltering, distancing, separating and focusing function of the house. Architecture gives a specific meaning to phenomena of nature and the elements in the same way that it gives a structure to human institutions, relations and behaviour.

Gaston Bachelard, whose phenomenological writings on the poetics of space and material imagination have inspired numerous studies in the mythopoetic basis of architecture during the past few decades, gives a monumental task to the house: '… [T]he house is one of the greatest powers of integration for the thoughts, memories and dreams of mankind', he argues.[2] Opposing the Heideggerian view of the fundamental anxiety in our human experience brought about by our being cast into the world, Bachelard argues that we are born in the context of architecture, and consequently our existential experience is always mediated and structured by architecture from the very beginning of our individual life. Even in the absence of a concrete house, the images of houses in our memory and imagination structure our experiences. In another context he elaborates his argument: 'All great, simple images reveal a psychic

state. The house, even more than the landscape, is a "psychic state" ... '[3]
Indeed, we do not confront the cosmos unprotected and unmediated as we
apply – consciously and unconsciously – perceived, remembered or imagined
architectural images to structure our experiences, thoughts and metaphors.
Through the ages architecture has provided one of the most efficient
metaphors for structure and order in human thought and imagination.

Architecture as metaphor

Architecture articulates the encounter of the world and the human mind. It
structures the 'flesh of the world' through spatial and material images that
articulate and give meaning to our basic human existential situations. An
architectural metaphor is a highly abstracted and condensed experiential
entity, which fuses the multiplicity of human experiences into a singular
lived image, or a sequence of such images. The ultimate condensations of
existential meaning are the images of one's room and home. The experience
of 'homeness' condenses our feelings of self, belonging, security and
meaning. Architecture arises from the concept and experience of home,
and even the multitude of other functions of buildings – work, gathering,
worship – derive from the mental essence of dwelling. Due to its primordial
significance, the house continues to be, poetically, the most potent design task
in architecture along with the buildings of belief and worship; earlier I argued
that architecture arises from the acts of dwelling and glorification. All powerful
artistic expressions in literature, music, painting and cinema alike are similar
existential condensations which are capable of communicating the complex
experience of being human instantaneously through a singular image.

Architectural metaphors or images have an extraordinary impact, due to their
structuring power, and they are even exploited in other art forms. Writers, for
instance, frequently relate their work to architectural structures and elements.
In her book *Dwelling in the Text,* Marilyn R Chandler writes:

> American writers as diverse as [Henry] James, [Willa] Cather, [Edith] Wharton
> and [William] Faulkner repeatedly use architectural metaphors to describe
> their work and their idea of the text as something that can best be understood
> spatially and structurally. In explaining their craft, they speak of surfaces and
> interiors, rooms and foyers, thresholds and windows, and furnishings. James,
> in perhaps the most famous of this conceit, likens the writer to a craftsman
> building a 'house of fiction' with 'a thousand windows'.[4]

The integrating power of the imagery of the house is well illustrated by the use of architectural settings and metaphors in literature. Chandler's book, for instance, is 'an exploration of the ways in which a number of our [American] major writers have appropriated houses as structural, psychological, metaphysical, and literary metaphors, constructing complex analogies between house and psyche, house and family structure, house and social environment, house and text'.[5] Architectural imagery has a similarly central role in cinema, theatre, photography and figurative painting. These images create the sense of context and place, as well as the culture and historical era, for the depicted scene or event.

Architecture as an organising image

The architectural image relates our experience of the world with the experience of our body through a process of unconscious internalisation, identification and projection. Genuine architectural structures strengthen our experience of the real, as well as horizontality and verticality, above and below, distant and near. Even the images and references of language are based on these bodily schemes, metaphors and images, as Mark Johnson and George Lakoff convincingly argue: 'Metaphor is pervasive in everyday life, not just in language but in thought and action. Our ordinary conceptual system, in terms of which we both think and act, is fundamentally metaphorical in nature.'[6]

Architecture is our primary instrument of orientation in the world; our home determines the ultimate meaning of interiority and exteriority, familiarity and unfamiliarity, homeness and being away. As an abstraction and condensation of the world, the architectural image is an interpretation and concretisation of an idealised order. The traditional village form of the nomadic Rendile tribe in Kenya reconstructs the image of their understanding of the primary cosmic and social orders every night. The collapsible-framed leather huts of the tribe are transported by camels, and every evening the women erect the structures in the same configuration: the huts are placed in a circular formation with a larger space towards the direction of the rising sun and the chief's hut opposite this opening; the mental model of the cosmos and their social hierarchy is thus rebuilt every day.

Heidegger describes the dialogue of a special architectural structure, the classic Greek temple, with its setting and the world at large as follows:

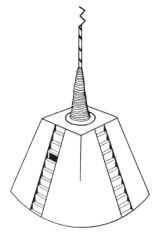

> Standing there, the building rests on the rocky ground. This resting of the work
> draws up out of the rock the mystery of that rock's clumsy yet spontaneous
> support. Standing there, the building holds its ground against the storm raging
> above it and so first makes the storm itself manifest in its violence.

The temple with its materiality makes visible otherwise invisible qualities of the
setting:

> The luster and gleam of the stone, though itself apparently glowing only by the
> grace of the sun, yet first brings to light the light of the day, the breadth of the
> sky, the darkness of the night. The temple's firm towering makes visible the
> invisible space of air. The steadfastness of the work contrasts with the surge of
> the surf, and its own repose brings out the raging of the sea.[7]

Heidegger further points out the mental effect of the temple as a special
framing device that even gives man his appropriate place: 'The temple, in its
standing there, first gives to things their look and then to men their outlook
on themselves.'[8] The world is experienced, sensed and assessed in relation to
the experiential base line of architecture. Architectural structures humanise the
world by giving it a human measure and a horizon of judgement and meaning.
They give a measure to the frightening infinity and homogeneity of cosmos.
At the same time that architecture creates a man-made nature, it also makes
natural phenomena manifest. Louis Kahn claims that architecture even makes

As Heidegger memorably
points out, the Greek temple
subconsciously organises the
experiential world, underlines
the characteristics of the
landscape and creates the
hierarchies between earth
and sky, mortals and gods.

The structure of the
imaginary Mythical Ark of the
Dogon is a similar magical
device that concretises the
memory of the creation of
the world and provides basic
hierarchies and classifications;
it is the concrete model
for the Dogon granary and
even includes the unit of
agricultural land in the square
unit at the top of the Ark.

The Acropolis, Athens,
Greece.

The temple marks an axis
mundi that frames the
landscape and provides
the experiential motives
for psychic and cultural
meanings.

Drawing of the Dogon
Mythical Ark based on
the verbal description of a
Dogon elder Ogotemmêli as
recorded by Marcel Griaule.

The circular base symbolises
the sun, the square roof the
sky, and the circle within it
the moon. The door to the
interior, containing two floors
and eight compartments, is
located on the sixth step of
the stair on the north side.

us fully aware of the miracle of the light of the sun: 'The sun never knows how great it is until it hits the side of a building or shines inside a room.'[9]

Like Heidegger and Bachelard, Karsten Harries sees the mental role of architecture in terms of providing the fundamental experiential order and meaning:

> Architecture helps to replace meaningless reality with a theatrically, or rather architecturally, transformed reality, which draws us in and, as we surrender to it, grants us an illusion of meaning [...] we cannot live with chaos. Chaos must be transformed into cosmos. [...] When we reduce the human need for shelter to material need, we lose sight of what we can call the ethical function of architecture.[10]

The philosopher points out the significance of this ethical function in the art of architecture; when architecture loses its contact with this essential mental ground, it turns into an empty exercise in technique and aestheticisation.

As opposed to the depicted, simulated or enacted imagery of the other art forms, architecture takes place in the real world of daily activities, in the actual theatre of life. Consequently, its ethical task is to be supportive of life and enhance our existential experience by providing it with a specific frame of understanding and meaning. The idea of architecture as a form of cultural critique that has been presented during recent decades is thus philosophically and ethically suspect. The task of architecture is not to shock, critique, amaze or entertain, but to provide us with our foothold in the realm of the real, and thus lay the foundation for a critical position to culture and life.

Architecture as a verb

The material building is not an object or end in itself. It alters and conditions our experiences of reality: a building frames and structures, articulates and relates, separates and unites, prohibits and facilitates. Deep architectural experiences are relations and acts rather than physical objects, or mere visual entities. As a consequence of this implied action, a bodily encounter with an architectural structure, space and light, is an inseparable aspect of the experience. Architectural images are promises and invitations: the floor is an invitation to stand up, establish stability and act, the door invites us to enter and pass through, the window to look out and see, the staircase to ascend and descend. The fireplace invites us to assemble around the life-supporting centre and gathering image of fire, the natural focus of domesticity and dreaming (illustration, page 129, Antonio Gaudí, Casa Battló, Barcelona, Spain 1904–06). Consequently, authentic experiential or mental elements of architecture are not visual units or geometric *gestalt*, as perceptually based post-Bauhaus theory and pedagogy have suggested, but *confrontations*, *encounters* and *acts* which project and articulate specific embodied and existential meanings. A building is encountered, not only viewed; it is approached, confronted, entered, related to one's body, moved about, and utilised as a context and condition for activities and things. A building directs, scales and frames actions, interrelations, perceptions and thoughts. Most importantly, it articulates our relations with other people as well as with the 'human institutions', to use a notion put forward by Louis Kahn. Architectural constructions concretise social, ideological, cultural and mental order by giving them metaphorical material form.

Consequently, the basic architectural experiences have the essence of *verbs* rather than *nouns*. Authentic architectural experiences consist, for example, of approaching the volume of the building, and sensing its physical presence, rather than the formal apprehension of the facade; the act of entering or crossing the boundary between two spatial realms, not the appreciation of the visual image of the door; looking out of the window and being reconnected with the world outside, rather than the window itself as a unit of visual design. The quality of a window lies in the manner in which it elaborates and expresses its 'windowness', how it mediates between outsideness and insideness, frames and scales the view, articulates light and privacy, and how it invigorates the room and gives it its special scale, rhythm and ambience (illustration, page 129, Caspar David Friedrich, *Woman at a Window*, 1822). Architecture turns a space into a specific place. It directs our attention away from itself; the window reveals the beauty of the courtyard and the tree outside, or it focuses on the distant silhouette of a mountain. A room can be terrifying or peaceful, aggressive or calming, imprisoning or liberating, dull or vivid, solely by means of the nature of its window. Thus, the impact of architecture on the human experience is too deeply existentially rooted to be approached solely as an element of visual design.

The house and the body

The authenticity and poetic power of an architectural encounter is founded on the tectonic language of construction and the comprehensibility of the act of construction by our senses. At the same time as a building speaks about the world through its embodied metaphor, it tells the story of its own construction, its own genesis, and it sets itself in a dialogue with the entire history of architecture; true architecture makes us remember other buildings. All meaningful buildings are simultaneously about the world, life and the discipline of architecture itself. In concretising the present, they evoke our awareness of the past, as well as our confidence in the future.

We behold, touch, listen and measure the world with our entire bodily constitution and existence, and the experiential world is organised and articulated around the centre of the body. In fact, our existential world has two simultaneous foci: our body and our home. There is a special dynamic relationship between the two; they can fuse and provide an ultimate sense of connectedness, or they may be distanced from each other, giving rise to a sense of longing, nostalgia and alienation. Our domicile is the refuge and projection of our body, memory and self-identity. We are in a constant dialogue and interaction with the environment, to the degree that it is impossible to detach the image of the self from its spatial and situational context. 'I am the space where I am,' as the poet Noël Arnaud put it.[11]

There is a vivid unconscious identification, resonance and correspondence between images of the house and our own body with its sense organs and metabolic functions. This is a two-way correspondence; the house is a metaphor of the body, and the body a metaphor of the house. The body–house relationship is often revealed by art works such as Louise Bourgeois's house–body images (illustration, page 126, Louise Bourgeois, *Femme Maison*). Experiencing a place, space or house is a dialogue, an exchange: I place myself in the space and the space settles in me. A humane building incorporates the scale, movement patterns and domains of the occupant and resonates with his/her presence and acts.

Rilke gives a touching description of the imagery of the internalised memory of the childhood house:

> Afterwards I never again saw that remarkable house [...] it is no complete building: it is all broken up inside me; here a room, there a room, and here a piece of hallway that does not connect these two rooms but is preserved, as a fragment, by itself.

The poet continues the description of the fragmented image:

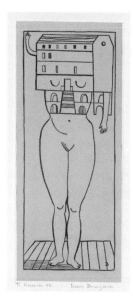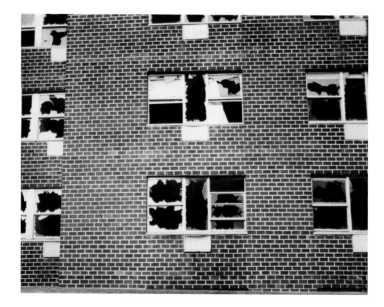

In this way it is all dispersed within me – the rooms, the stairways that descended with such ceremonious deliberation, and other narrow, spiral stairs in the obscurity of which one moved as blood does in the veins [...] all that is still in me and will never cease to be in me. It is as though the picture of this house had fallen into me from an infinite height and had shattered against my very ground.[12]

The poet's description illustrates the way the lived image of a house is an agglomeration of various detached images and recollections rather than a singular object or fixed picture.

Historicity of architectural images

CG Jung's record of one of his dreams provides a description of the mental historicity of the images of the house and their relation to the dweller's own mind and him/herself as a historical being:

It was [...] a house I did not know, which had two stories. It was 'my house' [...]
It was plain to me that the house represented a kind of image of psyche – that
is to say my then state of consciousness, with [...] unconscious additions.

ARCHITECTURE AND THE BODY

We have an unconscious tendency to associate aspects of the world with our body. These associations are revealed in dreams and artistic images, such as Louise Bourgeois' Woman Houses. Recent neurological studies have revealed that our capacity for affective experience and empathetic identification derives from our projective neural activities, such as 'mirror neurons'. Our unconscious interpretation of windows as the eyes of the house makes broken windows painfully appear as violated eyes. We tend to see buildings as 'creatures' with their distinct anatomical features.

Louise Bourgeois, *Femme Maison (Woman House)*, only state, 1984. New York, Museum of Modern Art (MoMA). Photogravure with chine collé, plate: 10 $^1/_{16}$ × 4 $^5/_{16}$" (25.6 × 11 cm).; sheet: 19 $^5/_{16}$ × 14 $^{15}/_{16}$" (49 × 38 cm). Gift of the artist.

Several works of Bourgeois reveal the unconscious association between the images of the human body and house.

Gordon Matta-Clark, *Window Blowout*, 1976, eight black and white photographs, vintage prints, baryta paper 26.8 × 34 cm each.

Broken windows are subliminally and painfully experienced as violated eyes because of our unconscious bodily identification.

Consciousness was represented by the salon. It had an inhabited atmosphere, in spite of its antique style.

Entering further floors below, the dream image is engaged with increasingly unconscious layers of the mind:

> The ground floor stood for the first level of the unconscious. The deeper I went, the more alien and darker the scene became. In the cave, I discovered remains of a primitive culture – that is, the world of the primitive man within myself – a world which can scarcely be reached or illuminated by consciousness. The primitive psyche of man borders on the life of the animal soul, just as the caves of prehistoric times were usually habited by animals before man laid claim to them.[13]

It is evident that a deep architectural experience cannot arise from an intellectualised concept, abstract formal idea, compositional refinement or a fabricated visual form. A moving and invigorating architectural experience arises from the reactivation of images concealed in our historicity as biological and cultural beings. Our relationship to the house also reflects characteristics of our personal histories, as we tend to search out the places where we have felt protected and happy and avoid situations that frightened us earlier in life. These experiences echo ageless experiences of safety, shelter, comfort and pleasure as well as the human relationship with the world at large. These arguments do not imply conservatism or looking backwards; my view is that *architecture needs to resonate with human historicity* in order to touch the deep ground of emotion and affect. We cannot be suddenly turned from biocultural beings into purely rational or aesthetic beings whose sensory and mental mechanisms could appreciate the world solely as an intellectual or aesthetic experience devoid of specific existential connotations. 'Understanding is not a quality coming to human reality from the outside; it is its characteristic way of existing,' as Sartre asserts.[14]

Our intense desire is to live in a world that makes existential sense. Without being regressive or historicist, authentic architectural images and metaphors re-articulate the primordial and historical essences of our existential experiences, concealed and stored in our genetic constitution and unconscious. A wall that moves us today echoes the first separation of the exterior and interior worlds; a roof that touches us makes us conscious of the climate and weather outside, and the pleasurable protection from the elements; the fireplace that gives us maximum comfort and pleasure today arises from the very invention of fire and the ageless enjoyment of the safety and domesticity of tamed fire by countless generations of our ancestors.

Bachelard points out that the house allows us to dream in safety, and it is difficult, indeed, to dream or think efficiently outdoors, as we need an enclosing and focusing room in order to think or dream in a concentrated manner. Architecture returns us to an innocent encounter with the world, at the same time that it mediates preconscious behavioural and mythical knowledge. The poetic essence of architecture is never stronger than when listening to the beating of heavy rain underneath a protecting roof, or when seeing a welcoming light in the window of one's house in the dark of a cold winter evening. The Fauvist painter Maurice de Vlaminck describes the primordial essence of the pleasure of the heat of the fireplace: 'The well-being I feel, seated in front of my fire, while bad weather rages out-of-doors, is entirely animal. A rat in its hole, a rabbit in its burrow, cows in the stable, must all feel the same contentment that I feel.'[15]

Primal architectural images and archetypes

The greatest mental effect and emotion in architecture is concentrated in distinct aspects, or confrontations with the house. These are not 'elements' in the sense of clearly delineated, defined and preconceived objects, or forms, as they are situations. As in the case of all artistic works, the ingredients of architectural experience derive their meaning from the entity, instead of the whole being grasped as the sum of its 'elements'. Architectural images, as all poetic images, obtain their mental impact through emotional and embodied channels before they are understood by the intellect. In fact, they may not be understood at all, and yet move us deeply. What is the 'meaning' of the Pantheon, Vierzehnheiligen, or Ronchamp, for instance? 'The richest experiences happen long before the soul takes notice. And when we begin to open our eyes to the visible, we have already been supporters of the invisible for a long time,' Gabriele d'Annunzio points out.[16]

The power of poetic and architectural images lies in their ability to condition the existential experience directly without conscious deliberation. In its very structure, the primary architectural image is akin to CG Jung's notion of the archetype that he developed on the basis of Sigmund Freud's idea of 'archaic remnants' which are part of the constitution of the human psyche. We still retain in our bodies physiological remnants of our aquatic life, a reminder of the horizontally blinking eyelid of our evolutionary reptilian phase, and the tail of our arboreal past. The archetypes are similar ancient mental or neural remnants. In accordance with Jung's definition, an archetype is not a specific meaning but

a tendency of an image to give rise to certain types of emotions, reactions and associations. In the same manner, architectural images do not project specific meanings, but give rise to certain experiences, feelings and associations. Instead of archetypes, Bachelard writes about 'primal images': 'I am going to try to characterize [...] primal images; images that bring out the primitiveness in us.'[17]

In the order of their ontological emergence, the primal images of architecture are: floor, roof, wall, door, window, hearth, stair, bed, table and bath. This view significantly assumes that architecture is born with the establishment of the floor, a horizontal surface, rather than the roof. As was pointed out earlier, profound architectural images are acts rather than formal entities or objects. These entities permit and invite: the floor invites movement, action and occupation; the roof projects shelter, protection and experiences of insideness; the wall signifies the separation of various realms and categories of spaces, and it creates, among other things, privacy and secrecy. Each one of the images can be analysed in terms of its ontology as well as its phenomenological essence.

Architectural experience arises ontologically from the act of inhabiting, and consequently, the primal architectural images can be most clearly identified in the context of the house, the human dwelling.

The categories that are usually deployed as foundational in analysing architecture, such as space, structure, scale, materiality or light, are surely important in the constitution and experience of architecture, but they are not primal architectural images. They are all relations and existential experiences of a composite nature articulated by architecture. This argument is a purely ontological view which does not intend to diminish the significance and expressive power of these aspects of architecture. They arise as elaborations and articulations of the primal images and they also exist outside and independently of the realm of architecture. Notions like space and light are generalised concepts and in accordance with the Bachelard quote in Chapter 2, 'Between concept and image there is no possibility of synthesis.'

The imagery of the window and the door

Various parts of the house have their resonance with the human body. Windows are the fragile eyes of the house, which observe the world and inspect visitors. A broken window is an unpleasant sight, arising from its unconscious association with a violated eye. The polarised and darkened window panes of contemporary buildings are houses blinded by some horrible and contagious illness; they are also malicious eyes that secretly control even the inhabitants themselves.

The eyes of the house pre-select and pre-view the landscape on behalf of human eyes. The landscapes and views, as framed and focused by the openings of the house, obtain a special intensity and meaning. The world seen through a window is a tamed and domesticated world. A view through a window has already been given a specific directionality, scale and meaning. The house provides protection for the dreamer, but only windows enable him/her to dream freely. We usually dream with closed or half-closed eyes and, in the same way, the window of a room of dreaming has to be shaded by curtains or closed with shutters. Dim light and unfocused vision stimulate dreaming and imagination. Yet, it is a forced situation to dream in a windowless space; the imagination is imprisoned and can only be set free with the possibility of view and light. It calls for a special power of concentration and intentionality to dream in a windowless cell. Human imagination desires sky and the horizon line.

Utility and habitability turn architecture into an act, an invitation, and give it a verb-like essence. The window frame is not an architectural experience, it is merely an experience of vision; looking through the window, and thus connecting two realms, inside and outside, turns the image into an authentic architectural experience. Caspar David Friedrich's painting *Woman at a Window*, 1822 (Nationalgalerie, Berlin), is thus a supreme lesson for architects on the 'windowness' of the window (illustration, page 129, left). The window as a device of mediation and the combined drama and sensuality of the mental transition from one domain to another is here memorably depicted; the interest in the physicality and 'thingness' of the window is replaced by the interest in the act of viewing. The mast of a boat even directs our consciousness to the joy of sailing and the vast horizon of the sea.

Similarly, the door and its frame, regardless of their possible visual splendour and craft skills, are not genuine architectural experiences, whereas entering through the door turns the experience into a profound architectural act. The history of painting offers countless images on the 'doorness' of the door.

A door is simultaneously a sign to halt and an invitation to enter. The front door of the house resists the body by its very weight, it ritualises the entry, and makes one anticipate the rooms and life behind it. The door silences, but it is simultaneously a sign of the concealed voices both outside and indoors. Opening a door is an intimate physical encounter between the house and the body; the body meets the mass, materiality and surface of the door, and the door handle, polished to a sheen by use through time, offers a welcoming and familiarising handshake.

In contrast, the automated glass doors of today make entry physically convenient, but strip the act of entry of all its existential meaning. Excessive convenience and functionalisation in general tend to dilute architectural meaning. Efficient central heating turns the fireplace into a mere visual luxury. This is why highly technologised settings tend to leave our emotions cold and distant, as they are unable to invite and stimulate our deep primal imagery. A proper door simultaneously protects and invites, it mediates gestures of secrecy and welcome, privacy and invitation, courtesy and dignity. 'How concrete everything becomes in the world of the spirit when an object, a mere door, can give images of hesitation, temptation, desire, security, welcome and respect,' Bachelard exclaims.[18]

Dilution of images

The very transparency of the contemporary door diminishes its image power; presence has turned into absence, solidity into transparency, and the door has become an absent wall or, perhaps, a window. This disappearance of doorness is an example of the dilution of architectural images, and the loss of their deep primal contents which is taking place in the modern world. The floor has lost its association with the ground and become an artificial horizontal plate which solely facilitates functional stacking. The roof has become another horizontal plane, identical with the floor plate, and lost its protective roofness, its creature-like crouching and benign gestures. The wall has given up its thickness, solidity, materiality, opacity and mystery, and turned into a mere weightless surface or immaterial transparency. The window has lost its focused gaze and turned into a transparent wall, a voyeurist device, the door has become a mere transparent opening that can no longer conceal and protect. The hearth has lost its essence as a source of enveloping warmth and family gathering, a space of intimate warmth, and it has turned into a mere framed picture – the cold fire of the contemporary house which is also experienced in the microwave oven of the kitchen. The stair has become merely a practical device which has forgotten the difference between up and down, ascent and descent, Heaven and Hell. The bed no longer has its essence as a secret and intimate space as it has turned into a horizontal open stage, and, finally, the table has given up its centring power, communality and sacredness, and declined into a prosaic plane for the hurried act of eating, devoid of communal or metaphysical reverberations.

Again, I am not making these remarks in order to promote nostalgia or pessimism, but to point out the mental ground of emotive impact in various architectural images. As TS Eliot wisely reminds us, tradition cannot be possessed, it has to be rediscovered and reinvented by each new generation.[19]

The fragile image

Our Western culture aspires to power and domination. This quest also characterises architecture that usually seeks a forceful image and impact. Referring to a philosophical method that does not aspire to totalise the multitude of human discourses into a single system, the Italian philosopher

Gianni Vattimo introduced the notions of 'weak ontology' and 'fragile thought' – *il pensiero debole* – in *The End of Modernity*.[20] Vattimo's idea seems to be related to Goethe's method of 'Delicate Empiricism' ('*Zarte Empirie*'), an effort 'to understand a thing's meaning through prolonged empathetic looking and understanding it grounded in direct experience'.[21] According to Vattimo, we can speak of a 'weak' or 'fragile' architecture, or perhaps, more precisely, of an architecture of weak structure and image, as opposed to an architecture of strong structure and image. Whereas the latter desires to impress us through an outstanding singular image and a consistent articulation of form, the architecture of weak image is contextual and responsive; it is concerned with sensory interaction instead of idealised and conceptual manifestations. This architecture grows and opens up, instead of the reverse process of closing down from the concept to the detail. Due to the negative connotations of the word 'weak', we should, perhaps, use the notion 'fragile architecture'.

In an essay entitled 'Weak Architecture',[22] Ignasi de Solà-Morales projects Vattimo's ideas on the reality of architecture somewhat differently from my interpretation, asserting that:

> In the field of aesthetics, literary, pictorial and architectonic experience can no longer be founded on the basis of a system: not a closed, economic system such as that of the classical age [...] the present-day artistic universe is perceived from experiences that are produced at discrete points, diverse, heterogeneous to the highest degree, and consequently our approximation to the aesthetic at every turn the possibility that it might ultimately be transformed definitively into a central experience.[23]

He defines 'event' as the fundamental ingredient of architecture and concludes his essay as follows: 'This is the strength of weakness; that strength which art and architecture are capable of producing precisely when they adopt a posture that is not aggressive and dominating, but tangential and weak.'[24]

We could equally speak of a 'weak urbanism'.[25] The dominant trends of town planning have also been based on strong strategies and strong urban form, usually based on geometry and axial composition, whereas the medieval townscapes, as well as the urban settings of traditional communities, have grown on the bases of weak and localised principles. The dominance of the eye reinforces strong strategies, whereas weak principles of urbanity give rise to a haptic townscape of intimacy and participation.

A similar 'weak structure' has also emerged in literature and cinema; the new French novel, *le nouveau roman*, deliberately fragments the linear progression of the story and opens it up to alternative interpretations. The films of Michelangelo Antonioni and Andrei Tarkovsky, similarly, exemplify a weak cinematic narrative, based on discontinuous narrative, straying camera and repeated improvisation. Such a technique creates a deliberate distance between the image and the narrative, with the intention of weakening the logic of the story and thus creating an associative field of clustered images. Instead of being an external spectator of the narrative event, the reader/viewer is made a participant, one who accepts a moral responsibility for the progression of the events.[26]

A distinct 'weakening' of the architectural image takes place through the processes of weathering and ruination. Erosion strips away a building's layers of utility, rational logic and detail articulation, and pushes the structure into the realm of uselessness, nostalgia and melancholy. The language of matter takes over from the visual and formal effect, and the structure attains a heightened intimacy. The arrogance of perfection is replaced by a humanising vulnerability. This is surely why artists, photographers, filmmakers and theatre directors tend to utilise images of eroded and abandoned architecture to evoke a subtle emotional atmosphere.

A similar weakening of architectural logic takes place in the reuse and renovation of buildings. The insertion of new functional and symbolic structures short-circuits the initial architectural logic of the structure and opens up unexpected and unorthodox emotional and expressive modes of experience. Architectural settings that layer contradictory ingredients usually project a special charm. Often the most enjoyable museum, office or residential space is that which is retrofitted into an adapted existing building.

The ecological approach also favours an adaptive image, parallel to the inherent weakness of ecologically adaptive processes. This ecological fragility is reflected in much contemporary art, for instance, in the poetic works of

Richard Long, Hamish Fulton, Wolfgang Laib, Andy Goldsworthy and Nils-Udo, all set in a subtle dialogue with nature. Here again, artists give an inspiring example for architects.

The art of gardening is an art form inherently engaged with time, change and the fragile image. On the other hand, the geometric garden exemplifies the attempt to domesticate nature into patterns of man-made geometry and order. The traditions of landscape and garden architecture provide an inspiration for an architecture liberated from the constraints of geometric and strong image. The biological models – varyingly called biomimicry, bionics and biophilia – have already entered various fields of science, medicine and engineering. Why should they not be valid in architecture?

The architecture of the Japanese garden, with its multitude of parallel, intertwining themes fused with nature, and its subtle juxtaposition of natural and man-made morphologies, is an inspiring example of the aesthetic power of weak form (illustration, page 43, Ryoan-ji kare-sansui Garden, The Temple of the Peaceful Dragon, Kyoto). The remarkably sensitive and stimulating architecture of Dimitris Pikionis's footpaths leading to the Acropolis in Athens (1954–7), the abstracted waterfall of Lawrence Halprin's Ira's Fountain (1970) in Portland, Oregon, and Carlo Scarpa's meticulously crafted architectural settings are contemporary examples of an architecture that places us in a different relation to space, form and time than the architecture of forceful geometry. These are examples of an architecture whose full power does not rely on a singular concept or image. Pikionis's work is a dense conversation with time and history to the extent that the design appears as a product of anonymous tradition or serendipity without drawing any attention to the individual creator (illustration, page 136, Dimitris Pikionis, Roadway, Filopáppos Hill, Athens, Greece). Halprin's designs explore the threshold between architecture and nature; they have the relaxed naturalness of scenes of nature, yet read as a man-made counterpoint to the geological and organic world (illustration, page 136, Lawrence Halprin, Auditorium Forecourt Plaza, Portland, Oregon, 1961). Scarpa's architecture creates a dialogue between concept and making, visuality and tactility, design and craft, artistic invention and tradition. Although his projects often seem to lack an overruling idea, they project an impressive and intense experience of architectural discovery and courtesy (illustration, page 72, Carlo Scarpa, Castelvecchio Museum, Verona).

The strong image in art aspires to the perfectly articulated and final artefact. This is the Albertian aesthetic ideal of perfection in the artistic work. By definition, a strong image has minimal tolerance for change and consequently contains an inherent aesthetic vulnerability in relation to the forces of time. A weak gestalt, on the other hand, allows additions and alterations; a fragile form possesses aesthetic tolerance, a margin for change. The criterion of tolerance also takes place on a psychological level; contemporary designs are often so constrained in their exclusive aesthetics that they create a hermetic and arrogant sense of isolation and autism, whereas a fragile image projects a welcoming open-endedness and a sense of aesthetic relaxation.

Through the process of design, the strong image is obliged to simplify and reduce the multiplicity of problems and practicalities in order to condense the shapeless diversity of aspects and requirements of the design task into a singular image. Such a strong image is often reached by means of severe functional and psychological censoring and suppression; the clarity of image contains frequently hidden repression.

John Ruskin believed that, 'Imperfection is in some way essential to all that we know of life. It is the sign of life in a mortal body, that is to say, of a state of process and change. Nothing that lives is, or can be, rigidly perfect; part of it is decaying, part nascent ... And in all things that live there are certain irregularities and deficiencies, which are not only signs of life but sources of

'FRAGILE' IMAGES IN
ARCHITECTURE

The tradition of Western
architecture has aimed at
awe-inspiring, controlling and
commanding images based
on the authority of geometric
language and logic of form.
Vernacular traditions around
the world usually evoke a
relaxed and unauthoritarian
ambience.

The history of modern and
contemporary architecture
also contains projects that are
based on a 'weak' or 'fragile'
formal elaboration. These
works invite us as participants
and open up spontaneous
architectural narratives.

Dimitris Pikionis, Roadway,
Filopáppos Hill, Athens,
Greece, 1954–7.

The design appears as an
accidental and unintentional
assembly of found stone
materials.

Lawrence Halprin, Auditorium
Forecourt Plaza, Portland,
Oregon, 1961.

The fountain is clearly man-
made in its geometry, but
at the same time, it projects
the serendipity, richness and
relaxed ambience of natural
settings.

beauty.'[27] Alvar Aalto elaborated Ruskin's idea when he spoke of 'the human error', or 'benign error', arguing that the human error has always been part of architecture. 'In a deeper sense, it has even been indispensable to making it possible for buildings to fully express the richness and positive values of life.'[28]

Architectural design usually aspires to a continuity of ideas and articulation throughout the project, whereas fragile imagery seeks deliberate discontinuities. Aalto's design process, for instance, produces differences and discontinuities instead of a unifying logic. Some of his finest buildings consist of distinct architectural episodes or events instead of following a single formal idea or logic throughout the project. Aalto was also a master in turning last minute design alterations, or mistakes made in the execution on the site, into brilliant detail improvisations. Such last-minute changes would not be possible in a design process based on closed logic.

Newness and tradition

Our current obsession with novelty and uniqueness as the sole criterion of architectural quality is detaching architecture from its mental and experiential ground and turning it into a production of fabricated visual imagery. Today's products of architectural virtuosity may amaze us, but they are usually unable to touch our soul because their expression is detached from the existential and primordial ground of human experience and it has lost its ontological ground and echo. The way to re-charge architectural images with emotive power is to reconnect them to their ontological essence and primal impact on the human mind. We need to think of 'the psyche of form', to use an expression of the young Alvar Aalto.[29]

Poetic imagery in music, poetry, painting and architecture alike arises from a timeless existential and experiential ground as seen and experienced through today's sensibilities. Art is fundamentally about the experience of being human and alive, instead of being an object of intellectual or formal speculation. Poetic images are not fabricated, they are encountered, revealed and re-articulated. That is why mere newness ends up being a shallow criterion for artistic quality.

Tradition is an astounding sedimentation of images and experiences, and it cannot be invented; it can only be lived. It constitutes an endless excavation of layered, internalised and shared myths, memories, images and experiences. Tradition is the site of the archaeology of emotions. An artistic image which does not derive from this mental soil is doomed to remain a mere rootless fabrication, a quotation from the encyclopaedia of formal inventions, and destined to wither away without being able to refertilise the soil and continuum of a renewed tradition, and thus become itself part of it. The artist or the architect needs to be in touch with the primordial and unconscious origins of poetic imagery in order to create images which can become part of our life, images that can touch us with the subtlety and freshness of authentic newness. 'In order to discover something new, we must study what is oldest,' my professor and mentor Aulis Blomstedt used to teach in the 1960s.[30] Louis Kahn likewise saw that creativity arises from the dialectics between the timeless and the timely.

References

1 Gaston Bachelard, *The Poetics of Space*, Beacon Press (Boston), 1969, p 46.
2 Ibid. p 6.
3 Ibid. p 72.
4 Marilyn R Chandler, *Dwelling in the Text: Houses in American Fiction*, University of California Press (Berkeley, Los Angeles, Oxford), 1991, p 2.
5 Ibid. p 3.
6 George Lakoff and Mark Johnson, *Metaphors We Live By*, University of Chicago Press (Chicago and London), 1980, p 3.
7 Martin Heidegger, *Poetry, Language, Thought*, Harper & Row (New York, Hagerstown, San Francisco, London), 1975, p 42.
8 Ibid. p 43.
9 Louis I Kahn, paraphrasing Wallace Stevens in 'Harmony Between Man and Architecture', *Louis I Kahn: Writings, Lectures, Interviews*, edited by Alessandra Latour, Rizzoli International Publications (New York), 1991, p 343.
10 Karsten Harries, 'Thoughts on a Non-Arbitrary Architecture', in David Seamon, editor, *Dwelling, Seeing and Designing: Toward a Phenomenological Ecology*, State University of New York Press (Albany), 1993, p 47.
11 As quoted in Bachelard, *The Poetics of Space*, 1969, 137.
12 Rainer Maria Rilke, *The Notebooks of Malte Laurids Brigge*, WW Norton & Company (New York and London), 1992, pp 30–1.
13 CG Jung's dream as published in Clare Cooper, 'The House as a Symbol of Self', in J Lang, C Burnette, W Moleski & D Vachon, editors, *Designing for Human Behavior*, Dowden, Hutchinson & Ross (Stroudsburg, PA), 1974, pp 40–41.
  Another version of the dream is given in Carl G Jung, 'Approaching the Unconscious', Carl G Jung et al, editors, *Man and His Symbols*, Laurel (New York), 1964, pp 42–3.
14 Jean-Paul Sartre, *The Emotions: Outline of a Theory*, Carol Publishing Group (New York), 1993, p 9.
15 As quoted in Bachelard, *The Poetics of Space*, 1969, p 91.
16 Gabriele d'Annunzio, *Contemplazione della morte*, Treves (Milan), 1912, pp 17–18.
17 Bachelard, *The Poetics of Space*, 1969, p 91.
18 Ibid. p 224.
19 TS Eliot, 'Tradition and the Individual Talent', *Selected Essays*, Harcourt, Brace & Company (New York), 1950.
20 Vattimo introduced the notion in the late 1970s. The idea was developed in a volume of essays entitled *Il pensiero debole* edited by Vattimo in collaboration with Pier Aldo Rovatti. Vattimo also discusses the notion in his book *The End of Modernity*, Johns Hopkins University Press (Baltimore, MD), 1991.
21 'There is a delicate empiricism which makes itself utterly identical with the object, thereby becoming true theory,' *Goethe: Scientific Studies*, Princeton University Press (New York), 1934, p 307.
22 Ignasi de Solà-Morales, *Differences: Topographies of Contemporary Architecture*, MIT Press (Cambridge, MA), 1997, pp 57–70.
23 Ibid. pp 58, 60.
24 Ibid. p 70.
25 Simon Hubacker, 'Weak Urbanism', *Daidalos 72* (1999), pp 10–17.
26 See, Juhani Pallasmaa, *The Architecture of Image: Existential Space in Cinema*, Rakennustieto Oy (Helsinki), 2001, pp 123–5.
27 John Ruskin, *The Lamp of Beauty: Writings on Art by John Ruskin*, Joan Evans, editor, Cornell University Press (Ithaca, NY), 1980, p 238.
28 Alvar Aalto, 'The Human Factor', in Göran Schildt, *Alvar Aalto in His Own Words*, Otava Publishing Company (Helsinki), 1997, p 281.
29 Alvar Aalto, 'Abbé Coignard's Sermon', in Göran Schildt, *Alvar Aalto In His Own Words*, 1997, p 57.
30 Aulis Blomstedt, Finnish architect and professor (1906–79). Blomstedt was Professor of Architecture at the Helsinki University of Technology in 1958–66.

Selected bibliography

Aumont, Jacques, *The Image*, British Film Institute (London), 1997.

Bachelard, Gaston, *Air and Dreams: An Essay on the Imagination of Movement* (1943), Dallas Institute Publications (Dallas, TX), 1988.

Bachelard, Gaston, *The Flame of a Candle* (1961), Dallas Institute Publications (Dallas, TX), 1988.

Bachelard, Gaston, *The Poetics of Reverie: Childhood, Language, and the Cosmos* (1960), Beacon Press (Boston), 1971.

Bachelard, Gaston, *The Poetics of Space* (1958), Beacon Press (Boston), 1969.

Bachelard, Gaston, *The Right to Dream* (1970), Dallas Institute Publications (Dallas, TX), 1983, fifth printing.

Bachelard, Gaston, *Water and Dreams: An Essay On the Imagination of Matter* (1942), Dallas Institute Publications (Dallas, TX), 1999, third printing.

Bachelard, Gaston, *On Poetic Imagination and Reverie*, translated and introduced by Colette Gaudin, Spring Publications (Dallas, TX), 1998, third printing.

Casey, Edward S, *Imagining: A Phenomenological Study*, Indiana University Press (Bloomington and London), 1976.

Damasio, Antonio R, *Descartes' Error: Emotion, Reason, and the Human Brain*, Harper Collins Publishers (New York), 1994.

Dewey, John, *Art As Experience* (1934), Perigee Books (New York), 1980.

Ehrenzweig, Anton, *The Hidden Order of Art* (1967), Paladin (Frogmore, St Albans), 1973.

Ehrenzweig, Anton, *The Psychoanalysis of Artistic Vision and Hearing: An Introduction to a Theory of Unconscious Perception* (1953), Sheldon Press (London), 1975, third edition.

Fish, William, *Philosophy of Perception: A Contemporary Introduction*, Routledge (New York and London), 2010.

Gallagher, Shaun and Zakavi, Dan, *The Phenomenological Mind: An Introduction to Philosophy of Mind and Cognitive Science*, Routledge (London and New York), 2008.

Gallagher, Shaun, *How the Body Shapes the Mind*, Clarendon Press (Oxford), 2006.

Gibbs, Raymond, W Jr, *Embodiment and Cognitive Science*, Cambridge University Press (Cambridge, New York, Melbourne, Madrid, Cape Town, Singapore, São Paulo), 2005.

Heidegger, Martin, *Poetry, Language, Thought* (1971), Harper & Row (New York, Hagerstown, San Francisco, London), 1975.

Hildebrand, Grant, *Origins of Architectural Pleasure*, University of California Press (Berkeley, Los Angeles, London), 1999.

Jung, Carl G, *Man and His Symbols*, Laurel Books (New York), 1968.

Kearney, Richard, *Poetics of Imagining: From Husserl to Lyotard*, Harper Collins Academic (London), 1991.

Kearney, Richard, *The Wake of Imagination*, Routledge (London), 1994.

Mallgrave, Harry Francis, *The Architect's Brain: Neuroscience, Creativity and Architecture*, John Wiley & Sons (Chichester, West Sussex), 2010.

McClatchy, JD, editor, *Poets on Painters*, University of California Press (Berkeley, Los Angeles, London), 1988.

Merleau-Ponty, Maurice, *The Visible and the Invisible*, Northwestern University Press (Evanston, IL), 1968.

Modell, Arnold H, *Imagination and the Meaningful Brain*, MIT Press (Cambridge, MA and London, UK), 2006.

Onians, John, *Neuroarthistory: From Aristotle and Pliny to Baxandall and Zeki*, Yale University Press (New Haven and London), 2007.

Rentschler Ingo, Herzberger, Barbara, and Epstein, David, *Beauty and the Brain in Biological Aspects of Aesthetics*, Birkhäuser (Basel), 1988.

Sartre, Jean-Paul, *Imagination: A Psychological Critique* (1936), The University of Michigan Press (Ann Arbor), 1972.

Sartre, Jean-Paul, *The Emotions: Outline of a Theory* (1948), Carol Publishing Group (New York), 1993.

Sartre, Jean-Paul, *The Imaginary* (1940), Routledge (London and New York), 2010.

Sartre, Jean-Paul, *The Psychology of Imagination*, Citadel Press (Secaucus, NJ), 1948.

Scarry, Elaine, *Dreaming by the Book*, Princeton University Press (Princeton, NJ), 2001.

Strømnes, Frode J, *The Fall of the Word and the Rise of the Mental Model*, Peter Lang (Frankfurt am Main), 2006.

Varela, Francisco J, Thompson, Evan, and Rosch, Eleanor, *The Embodied Mind: Cognitive Science and Human Experience*, MIT Press (Cambridge, MA and London, UK), 1993.

Wilson, Edward O, *Biophilia: The Human Bond with Other Species*, Harvard University Press (Cambridge, MA and London, UK), 1984.

Zeki, Semir, *Inner Vision: An Exploration of Art and the Brain*, Oxford University Press (Oxford), 1999.

An embodied image that directly addresses our muscular and skeletal system. The sawatari-ishi, 'steps across marsh', in the garden of the Heian Shrine in Kyoto.

Index

Image credits

l= left, r = right, t= top, b= bottom

Cover image © ADAGP, Paris and DACS, London 2010

p 21 (l) © Peter Newark Military Pictures/The Bridgeman Art Library
p 21 (r) © Sigurdur Gudmundsson, courtesy of the artist and i8 gallery
p 27 (l) © Claudio Abate, Rome
p 27 (r) © ADAGP, Paris and DACS, London, 2010
p 30 (l) © Summerfield Press/Corbis
p 30 (r) The Art of Painting, c 1666–67 (oil on canvas) by Vermeer, Jan (1632–75)
Kunsthistorisches Museum, Vienna, Austria / The Bridgeman Art Library
Nationality / copyright status: Dutch / out of copyright
p 33 (l) © Digital image, The Museum of Modern Art, New York/Scala, Florence, 2010
p 33 (r) © Natural History Museum, Vienna or NHM, Vienna
p 43 (l) © Digital image, The Museum of Modern Art, New York/Scala, Florence, 2010 and
ADAGP, Paris and DACS, London 2010.
p 43 (r) © Michael S. Yamashita/Corbis
p 45 (l) © The Gallery Collection/Corbis
p 45 (r) © Giraudon / The Bridgeman Art Library and ADAGP, Paris and DACS, London 2010
p 47 (l) © David Churchill/Arcaid/Corbis
p 47 (r) © Andrey A Tarkovsky
p 49 (l) © Laleh Bakhtiar
p 49 (r) © Sigurdur Gudmundsson, courtesy of the artist and i8 gallery
p 52 (l) © The Bridgeman Art Library, ADAGP, Paris and DACS, London 2010
p 52 (r) © Rauno Träskelin
p 56 (l) © Bettmann/Corbis
p 56 (r) © The Bridgeman Art Gallery
p 59 (tr) © FLC/DACS 2010
p 59 (b) © DACS 2010
p 62 (l) © Alen MacWeeney/Corbis
p 62 (r) © Louis I. Kahn Collection, The University of Pennsylvania and the Pennsylvania
Historical and Museum Commission
p 69 (l) © Collection of Sue Ann Kahn
p 69 (r) © Andrew Holbrooke/Corbis
p 70 (r) © Gustaf Welin, Alvar Aalto Museum, 1930s
p 72 (l) © Martin Hecl
p 72 (r) © Klaus Frahm/arturimages
p 74 (l) © By courtesy of the Trustees of Sir John Soane's Museum
p 74 (r) © Rauno Träskelin